Happy Birthday to You!
Happy Birthday to You!
Happy Birthday, Dear

....

Happy Birthday to You!
From:

....

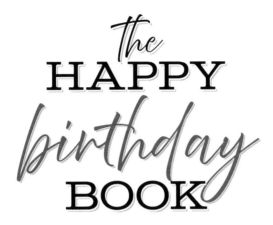

the HAPPY birthday BOOK

A CELEBRATION OF YOU!

CHARLES L. ALLEN AND
MILDRED F. PARKER

W PUBLISHING GROUP

AN IMPRINT OF THOMAS NELSON

ISBN 978-1-4003-3275-5 (hardcover)
ISBN 978-1-4003-3454-4 (eBook)

Library of Congress Cataloging-in-Publication Data on File

Printed in China
23 24 25 26 27 GRI 6 5 4 3 2 1

CONTENTS

THE *Most Sung* SONG

The song that is sung more than any other in all the world is "Happy Birthday to You."

Birthdays are very special to all of us. It is a time to express appreciation for those we love and care about.

It was Amos Bronson Alcott who said, "Of gifts, there seems none more becoming to offer a friend than a beautiful book. And Richard Braunstein said, "It is possible to give with loving, but it is impossible to love without giving."

We planned *The Happy Birthday Book* as a gift for that special person on that special day. We hope you enjoy it for years to come.

CHARLES L. ALLEN
MILDRED F. PARKER

PART 1

*Your Day to
Celebrate!*

Chapter 1
BIRTHDAYS

The first fact about the celebration of a birthday is that it is a way of affirming defiantly, and even flamboyantly, that it is a good thing to be alive.

G. K. CHESTERTON

A Birthday marks a unit of time.
Some use it to reflect on the past,
Others as a dream for the future—
As for me, I'll rejoice in the present.

MILDRED PARKER

*This day I am, by blessing of God,
34 years old, in very good health and
mind's content. . . . The Lord's name be
praised! and may I be thankful for it.*

SAMUEL PEPYS, DIARY ENTRY ON HIS BIRTHDAY, FEBRUARY 23, 1667

*Sad? Why should I be sad? It's my birthday.
The happiest day of the year.*

EEYORE IN A. A. MILNE'S *WINNIE-THE-POOH*

Pleas'd to look forward, pleas'd to look behind.
And count each birthday with a grateful mind.

ALEXANDER POPE

A Birthday

My heart is like a singing bird
    Whose nest is in a watered shoot;
My heart is like an apple-tree
    Whose boughs are bent with thick-set fruit;
My heart is like a rainbow shell
    That paddles in a halcyon sea;
My heart is gladder than all these,
    Because my love is come to me.

Raise me a dais of silk and down;
    Hang it with vair and purple dyes;
Carve it in doves and pomegranates,
    And peacocks with a hundred eyes;
Work it in gold and silver grapes,
    In leaves and silver fleur-de-lys;
Because the birthday of my life
    Is come, my love is come to me.

CHRISTINA ROSSETTI

What different dooms our birthdays bring!

THOMAS HOOD

Monday's child is fair of face,
Tuesday's child is full of grace,
Wednesday's child is full of woe,
Thursday's child has far to go,
Friday's child is loving and giving,
Saturday's child works for its living,
And a child that's born on the Sabbath day
Is fair and wise and good and gay.

AUTHOR UNKNOWN, PUBLISHED IN ST. NICHOLAS MAGAZINE (1873)

*If he had only kept his birthday, he might have
kept many other things along with it.*

G. K. CHESTERTON, OF A FAMOUS WRITER WHO
REFUSED TO CELEBRATE HIS OWN BIRTHDAY

A Birthday in a family
Is a time of celebration:
Ice cream and cake and candles
Gift-giving and laughter.

Such celebrations
Help us to put down roots
To know that we are loved
Ah! Happy Birthday to you!

MILDRED PARKER

Birthdays are nice to have, but too
many of them will kill a person!

May your birthday be hopeful, for hope is sure to
come right if only we go on hoping long enough.

GEORGE MACDONALD, LETTER TO HIS WIFE, 1877

A diplomatic husband said to his wife, "How
do you expect me to remember your birthday
when you never look any older?"

There was a sweet woman
Who lived in a shoe
She had had so many birthdays
She didn't know what to do.

She looked in her mirror,
Then made a quick decision
To devote more of her time
To being a perfect vision.

MILDRED PARKER

You know you are getting old when the
candles cost more than the cake.

BOB HOPE

Let's have one other gaudy night . . .
It is my birthday.

WILLIAM SHAKESPEARE, *ANTONY AND CLEOPATRA*

The saddest part of birthdays,
There really is no doubt,
Is each year I've more candles
And less breath to blow them out.

DONNA EVLETH

Birthday Prayer for a Child

Keep this little light, O Father,
Burning year on year—
Driving back the dark about it
With its rays of cheer.

Keep these little feet, O Father,
Standing here to-day
By the side of life's first mile-stone,
Always in Thy way.

Keep this little heart, O Father,
Loving, pure, and true,
That when come the evening shadows
Naught shall be to rue.

Keep this little one, O Father,
Near me through life's task—
In His name, who blessed the children,
This I humbly ask.

JOHN FINLEY[1]

Fourscore Years

My hands are gnarled, and my hair is gray
And I'm just eighty years old today.
My friends are coming my hand to shake,
My children are bringing a birthday cake.
A candle for every year?—Ah no,
A cake can hold but thirty or so.

Yet I shall enjoy the thoughts they bring,
The ties and socks, and the songs they sing.
Eighty years have passed me since my birth,
A right long time to be here on earth.
I'm tired and I've had almost enough.
Life hasn't been easy—the road was rough.

Yet I know as I 'wait Time's knock on my door,
I'd like to remain a year or two more,
To see what becomes of my Billy and Bess,
But the chances are slim that I may, I guess.
With the back of my hand, I brush a tear
As I open a well-worn book that's near.

There I see on a page once turned down by my
      wife
"I come that you may have eternal life."
And then turning over a page or two—
"I go to prepare a place for you."
Once more I turn, and the lines now say—
"For a thousand years are but a day."

Old Book, you've never been known to be wrong,
And according to you, I've not lived very long.
So, I get out my pencil and soon it is clear
Though I've spent eighty years on this earthly
      sphere,
Though they've worn my body and stiffened my
      knee
Yet I'm but two hours old in eternity!

So, at last I know, though my frame is old,
Though my eyes are dim, and my hands are cold,
Why it is that inside I'm still young enough
      to play—
It's because I'm just starting on my way:
A babe in the eyes of time to be,
Just two hours old in Eternity!

AUTHOR UNKNOWN

Leap Year

The twenty-ninth of February! It is a great day; at least, it is a great day for some people. It is a very great day for my little friend, Beryl Burleigh, who suffered the misfortune to be born on that rarely recurring date. Beryl is in excellent company, if that is any consolation to her. Among many other distinguished people, I find that John Whitgift, a very celebrated Archbishop of Canterbury, and John Byrom, who composed our National Anthem and some of our best-known hymns, shared with Beryl the distinction of enjoying a birthday only once in four years. In the careers of all of these famous men there was a time when they went to bed with sad thoughts on the night of the twenty-eighth of February, and woke up with still sadder ones on the morning of the first of March.

F. W. BOREHAM[2]

So you may live in honor, as in name,
If with this truth you be inspir'd,
So may
This day
Be more, and long desir'd:
And with the flame
Of love be bright,
As with the light
Of bone-fires. Then
The Birth-day shines. . . .

BEN JONSON, "ODE TO SIR WILLIAM SYDNEY, ON HIS BIRTHDAY"

For some ridiculous reason, to which, however,
    I've no desire to be disloyal,
Some person in authority, I don't know who, very
    likely the Astronomer Royal,
Has decided that, although for such a beastly
    month as February twenty-eight days as a
    rule are plenty,
One year in every four his days shall be reckoned
    as nine-and-twenty.
Through some singular coincidence—I shouldn't
    be surprised if it were owning to the agency
    of an ill-natured fairy—
You are the victim of this clumsy arrangement,
    having been born in leap-year, on the
    twenty-ninth of February,
And so, by a simple arithmetical process, you'll
    easily discover,
That though you've lived twenty-one years, yet,
    if we go by birthdays, you're only five and a
    little bit over!

W. S. GILBERT, *THE PIRATES OF PENZANCE*

Precious Gems

Each birthday's like a precious gem
    That brings its beauty rare;
A treasured jewel that makes you feel
    like you're a millionaire.

The years are like bright emeralds,
    The months are rubies red,
The weeks are like a string of pearls
    Strung on a silver thread.

The days are sometimes sapphire clear,
    Or bright as opals fair,
And now and then there comes a day
    That's like a diamond rare.

The hours are like a chain of gold,
    Each link a vital part,
Binding these priceless jewels into
    A treasure for the heart.

So may the years that come to you
    Such happiness contain
That all the moments, days, and years
    Become a jeweled chain.

AUTHOR UNKNOWN

Heaven give you many, many merry days!

WILLIAM SHAKESPEARE

William Willimon tells about a boy's fourth birthday. His name is Clayton. Clayton's mother told him he could have any kind of birthday party he wanted, so Clayton said he wanted a party where everybody was a king or a queen. His wish was granted, and his mother set to work making all the costumes for the party. She made golden crowns from cardboard, robes out of crepe paper, and scepters for the kings and queens out of hangers.

The day of the party arrived, and as each guest arrived he or she was given a costume. Everyone at that party was either a king or a queen, and everyone had a great time. After cake and ice cream, they went outside and made a royal procession all the way to the end of the block and back again. All looked like kings and queens. And most importantly, all behaved like kings and queens, that is, with dignity and a sense of importance.

That night when the guests had all gone home and Clayton's mother was tucking him in bed, he said, "I wish everyone in the whole world could be a king or a queen not just on my birthday but every day."

MARK TROTTER[3]

PART 2

Happy Birthday to You!

Chapter 2
HAPPY

It is a Christian duty, as you know, for
everyone to be as happy as he can.

C. S. LEWIS

*The grand essentials for happiness are: something to
do, something to love, and something to hope for.*

THOMAS CHALMERS

Happiness is no laughing matter.

RICHARD WHATELY

Most folks are about as happy as they
make up their minds to be.

ABRAHAM LINCOLN

*All the Constitution guarantees is the pursuit of
happiness. You have to catch up with it yourself.*

The crowning fortune of a man is to be born to some pursuit
which finds him employment and happiness, whether it be to
make baskets or broadswords, or canals, or statues, or songs.

RALPH WALDO EMERSON

Happiness is not perfected until it is shared.

JANE PORTER

*All who would win joy, must share
it; happiness was born a twin.*

GEORGE GORDON, LORD BYRON

*The foolish man seeks happiness in the
distance; the wise grows it under his feet.*

JAMES OPPENHEIM

A little thought will show you how vastly your own happiness depends on the way other people bear themselves toward you. The looks and tones at your breakfast table, the conduct of your fellow workers or employers, the faithful or unreliable men you deal with, what people say to you on the street, the letters you get, the friends or foes you meet—these things make up very much of the pleasure or misery of your day. Turn the idea around, and remember that just so much are you adding to the pleasure or the misery of other people's days. And this is the half of the matter which you can control. Whether any particular day shall bring to you more of happiness or of suffering is largely beyond your power to determine. Whether each day of your life shall give happiness or suffering rests with yourself.

GEORGE S. MERRIAM

The art of living does not consist in preserving and clinging to a particular mood of happiness, but in allowing happiness to change its form without being disappointed by the change, for happiness, like a child, must be allowed to grow up.

CHARLES L. MORGAN

A man has no more right to consume happiness without producing some, than to consume goods without producing some.

EUGENE P. BERTIN

A happy man or woman is a better thing to find than a five-pound note. He or she is a radiating focus of good will; and their entrance into a room is as though another candle had been lighted.

ROBERT LOUIS STEVENSON

It is a Christian duty, as you know, for everyone to be as happy as he can.

C. S. LEWIS

To make happiness the goal of life is a commendable one and not selfish and self-centered. Happy individuals are healthier both mentally and physically. They make better students, better soldiers, better wives and husbands and parents. And because happiness is difficult to contain, the happy person sweetens and enriches every life he touches.

MARGARET E. MULAC

*Leaves seem light, useless, idle, wavering, and
changeable—they even dance; yet God has
made them part of the oak.—So he has given us
a lesson, not to deny stout-heartedness within,
because we see lightsomeness without.*

LEIGH HUNT

Your plan for work and happiness should be big, imaginative
and daring. Strike out boldly for the things you honestly want
more than anything else in the world. The mistake is to put
your sights too low, not to raise them too high.

HENRY J. KAISER

*The capacity for happiness is the most valuable
trait parents should nurture in their children.*

CHARLES WERTENBAKER

Let us be determined to be happy; make the most of the blessings that come to us; look on the bright side of everything.
Cheerfulness is not always spontaneous; but bears cultivation.
One who can carry a smiling face through a world where there
are so many troubled hearts, may unconsciously be a public
benefactor; for 'the merry heart doeth good like a medicine,'
and not alone to its possessor.

M. P. WELLS

There is no duty we so much underrate as the duty of being happy. By being happy, we sow anonymous benefits upon the world, which remain unknown even to ourselves, or when they are disclosed, surprise nobody so much as the benefactor.

ROBERT LOUIS STEVENSON

It takes wit and interest and energy to be happy. The pursuit of happiness is a great activity. One must be open and alive. It is the greatest feat men and women have to accomplish. . . . There must be courage. There are no easy ruts to get into which lead to happiness. Men and women must become interesting to themselves and must become actually expressive before they can be happy.

ROBERT HENRI

Happiness is rarely absent; it is that we don't recognize its presence.

Happiness consists more in small conveniences or pleasures that occur every day, than in great pieces of good fortune that happen but seldom to a man in the course of his life.

BENJAMIN FRANKLIN

A happy life is not built up of tours abroad and pleasant holidays, but of little clumps of violets noticed by the roadside, hidden away almost so that only those can see them who have God's peace and love in their hearts; in one long continuous chain of little joys, little whispers from the spiritual world, and little gleams of sunshine on our daily work.

EDWARD WILSON

The happiness of life is made up of minute fractions—the little soon-forgotten charities of a kiss or smile, a kind look, a heartfelt compliment, and the countless infinitesimals of pleasurable and genial feeling.

SAMUEL TAYLOR COLERIDGE

[Humankind] is always happier for having been happy; so that if you make them happy now you make them happy twenty years hence, by the memory of it.

SYDNEY SMITH

A happy life must be to a great extent a quiet life, for it is only in an atmosphere of quiet that true joy can live.

BERTRAND RUSSELL

Where your pleasure is, there is your treasure;
where your treasure, there your heart;
where your heart, there your happiness.

SAINT AUGUSTINE

Harry Emerson Fosdick repeated it again in the twentieth century: "Happiness is not mostly pleasure; it is mostly victory." Yes, the victory that comes from a sense of achievement, of triumph, of turning our lemons into lemonades.

DALE CARNEGIE

Happiness is not pleasure, and it is not getting what
you want; it is not smiling and it is not laughter. It
is a by-product of a life usefully lived, and there can
be no true happiness apart from true usefulness.

WALTER ROWE COURTNAY

If you ever find happiness by hunting for it,
you will find it as the old woman did her lost
spectacles, safe on her nose all the time.

JOSH BILLINGS

Do not run after happiness, but seek to do good, and you will find that happiness will run after you. The day will dawn full of expectation, the night will fall full of repose. This world will seem a very good place, and the world to come a better place still.

JAMES FREEMAN CLARK

Biblical Keys to Happiness

A merry heart does good, like medicine.

PROVERBS 17:22

It was right that we should make merry and be glad.

LUKE 15:32

Cast your burden on the LORD,
And He shall sustain you.

PSALMS 55:22

Do not worry.

MATTHEW 6:31 NLV

He has sent Me to heal the
brokenhearted, . . .
To comfort all who mourn, . . .
To give them beauty for ashes,
The oil of joy for mourning,
The garment of praise for the
spirit of heaviness;

ISAIAH 61:1–3

If you know these things, you
will be happy if you do them.

JOHN 13:17 NLV

In the Sermon on the Mount, Jesus promised his disciples three things—that they would be entirely fearless, that they would be absurdly happy, and that they would get into trouble. They did get into trouble and found, to their surprise, that they were not afraid. They were absurdly happy, for they laughed over their own troubles, and only cried over other people's.

W. R. MALTBY

If you observe really happy persons, you will find them building a boat, writing a symphony, educating children, growing double dahlias, or looking for dinosaur eggs in the Gobi desert. They will not be searching for happiness as if it were a collar button that had rolled under the radiator, striving for it as the goal itself. They will have become aware that they are happy in the course of living life twenty-four crowded hours of each day.

W. BÉRAN WOLFE

One thing I know; the only ones among you who will be really happy are those who will have sought and found how to serve.

ALBERT SCHWEITZER

Happiness does not depend upon a full pocketbook, but upon a mind full of rich thoughts and a heart full of rich emotions. It is measured by the spirit in which we meet the problems of life. This Hindu proverb gives us a clue: "Help thy brother's boat across the stream, and lo! thine own has reached the shore."

GOLDEN BONDURANT HOLLAND

Getters generally don't get happiness; givers get it. You simply give to others a bit of yourself—a thoughtful act, a helpful idea, a word of appreciation, a lift over a rough spot, a sense of understanding, a timely suggestion. You take something out of your mind, garnished in kindness out of your heart, and put it into the other fellow's mind and heart.

CHARLES H. BURR

The principles we live by, in business and in social life, are the most important part of happiness. We need to be careful, upon achieving happiness, not to lose the virtues which have produced it.

HARRY HARRISON

Half the world is on the wrong scent in the pursuit of happiness. They think it consists in having and getting, and in being served by others. On the contrary, it consists in giving, and in serving others.

HENRY DRUMMOND

The really happy person is one who can enjoy the scenery on a detour.

The most infectiously joyous men and women are those who forget themselves in thinking about others and serving others. Happiness comes not by deliberately courting and wooing it but by giving oneself in self-effacing surrender to great values.

ROBERT J. MCCRACKEN

The London Tablet asked this question: Who are the happiest people on earth? These were the answers: a craftsman or artist whistling over a job well done; a little child building sand castles; a mother, after a busy day, bathing her baby; and a doctor who has finished a difficult and dangerous operation and saved a human life.

GEORGE F. RILEY

We may scatter the seed of courtesy and kindness about us at little expense. Some of them will fall on good ground, and grow up into benevolence in the minds of others, and all of them will bear fruit of happiness in the bosom whence they spring.

JEREMY BENTHAM

No task is as difficult as striving to become a civilized person. But the lasting happiness which comes with that attempt makes the effort seem small indeed as compared with the value to be gained.

LELAND P. STEWART

I believe the recipe for happiness to be just enough money to pay the monthly bills you acquire, a little surplus to give you confidence, a little too much work each day, enthusiasm for your work, a substantial share of good health, a couple of real friends, and [loved ones] to share life's beauty with you.

J. KENFIELD MORLEY

If we would keep filling our minds with the picture of happy things ahead, many of the worries and anxieties, and perhaps ill health, would naturally melt away. . . . If we lived in the atmosphere of expectancy, so many of our petty problems would be no problems at all! Always expect the best. Then if you have to hurdle a few tough problems, you will have generated the strength and courage to do so. Successful businesses are forever planning and dreaming ahead. And so should we, as individuals. . . . Expect to discover the best in people and they will do the same for you. We must be constructive in our thoughts and our attitude toward life.

GEORGE MATTHEW ADAMS

The supreme happiness of life is the
conviction that we are loved.

VICTOR HUGO

No matter what looms ahead, if you can eat today, enjoy the sunlight today, mix good cheer with friends today, enjoy it and bless God for it. Do not look back on happiness—or dream of it in the future. You are only sure of today; do not let yourself be cheated out of it.

HENRY WARD BEECHER

If one only wished to be happy, this could be easily
accomplished; but we wish to be happier than
other people, and this is always difficult, for we
believe others to be happier than they are.

MONTESQUIEU

To be happy at home is the ultimate
result of all ambition.

SAMUEL JOHNSON

To take life for granted, grudgingly, is to spoil it; whereas to take it for gratitude, bravely and without fear, is to enjoy it, despite all its aches and ills. To be happy is easy enough if we give ourselves, forgive others, and live with thanksgiving. No self-centered person, no ungrateful soul can ever be happy.

ELTON TRUEBLOOD

It is an illusion to think that more comfort
means more happiness. Happiness comes of
the capacity to feel deeply, to enjoy simply,
to think freely, to risk life, to be needed.

STORM JAMESON

In every individual there is a great power for happiness that can be realized. But in many only a little trickle of that potential power gets through. The big secret in this day and age, as in past decades, is to get that power in mind and personality. This can change you into a person of effectiveness and happiness. This is the art of living, or indeed some of it.

NORMAN VINCENT PEALE

Happiness at its deepest and best is not the portion of a cushioned life which never struggled, overpassed obstacles, bore hardships, or adventured in sacrifice for costly aims. A heart of joy is never found in luxuriously coddled lives, but in men and women who achieve and dare, who have tried their powers against antagonisms, who have met even sickness and bereavement and have tempered their souls in fire. Joy is begotten not chiefly from the impression of happy circumstances, but from the expression of overcoming power. If we were set upon making a happy world, then, we could not leave struggle out nor make adversity impossible. The unhappiest world conceivable by man would be a world with nothing hard to do, no conflicts to wage for ends worthwhile; a world where courage was not needed and sacrifice was a superfluity.

HARRY EMERSON FOSDICK

An [elderly wise man] was approached by a visitor who said: "I observe your old and happy life. How do you attain it?" The old philosopher replied: "You see also the fine trees and orchards I possess. Well, I have them because I planted them as a young man. So in youth I laid the foundations of my life. I did not wait until I was old to begin to build for this day."

FRED R. CHENAULT

When asked to write a message on the flyleaf of a Bible, George V wrote: "The secret of happiness is not to do what you like to do, but to learn to like what you have to do."

JAMES GORDON GILKEY

The hand that in life grips with a miser's clutch,
and the ear that refuses to heed the pleading
voice of humanity forfeit the most precious of
all gifts of earth and of heaven—the happiness
that comes of doing good to others.

AMON G. CARTER

No one, I am convinced, can be happy who lives only for himself. The joy of living comes from immersion in something . . . that we know to be better, more enduring and worthier than we are. People; ideas; causes; above all, continuities—these offer the one possible escape not merely from selfishness but from the hungers of solitude and the sorrows of aimlessness. . . . The only true happiness comes from squandering ourselves for a purpose.

JOHN MASON BROWN

If anyone would tell you the shortest, surest
way to happiness and all perfection, he must
tell you to make it a rule to yourself to thank
and praise God for everything that happens to
you. For it is certain that whatever seeming
calamity happens to you, if you thank and
praise God for it, you turn it into a blessing.

WILLIAM LAW

One day a mountaineer invited a friend to climb with him to the top of a high peak. There they beheld a gorgeous sunset. The friend turned to the mountaineer and said: "Why are you crying?" The reply was: "All these years I have come here alone and filled my soul with this cup of God. Today I am happier than I have ever been, for this is the first time I have shared the glory with someone else."

If thou goest here and there seeking thine own will, thou shalt never be happy or free from care.

THOMAS Á KEMPIS

Don't mistake pleasure for happiness.
They are different breeds of dogs.

JOSH BILLINGS

We must dare to be happy, and dare to confess it, regarding ourselves always as the depositories, not as the authors of our own joy.

HENRI AMIEL

Chapter 3
BIRTH

God makes the world all over again,
whenever a little child is born.

JEAN PAUL RICHTER

To everything there is a season,
A time for every purpose under heaven.

A time to be born.

ECCLESIASTES 3:1

*Life is a flame that is always burning itself out, but
it catches fire again every time a child is born.*

GEORGE BERNARD SHAW

*An endless process of births is the perpetual answer of life
to the fact of death. It says that life keeps coming on, keeps
seeking to fulfill itself, keeps affirming the margin of hope
in the presence of desolation, pestilence and despair.*

HOWARD THURMAN

Birth is the sudden opening of a window, through which you look out upon a stupendous prospect. For what has happened? A miracle. You have exchanged nothing for the possibility of everything.

WILLIAM MACNEILE DIXON

Every child comes with the message that God is not yet discouraged of man.

RABINDRANATH TAGORE

We were born to inquire after truth.

MICHEL DE MONTAIGNE

In the first minute that my soul is infused, the Image of God is imprinted in my soul; so forward is God in my behalf, and so early does he visit me. But yet Original sin is there, as soon as the Image of God is there. My soul is capable of God, as soon as it is capable of sin.

JOHN DONNE

It is better to be nobly remembered, than nobly born.

JOHN RUSKIN

High birth is a thing which I never knew anyone to disparage except those who had it not; and I never knew anyone to make boast of it who had anything else to be proud of.

WILLIAM WARBURTON

There are two events over which we have little control,
birth and death, but we can enjoy the interval between.

GEORGE SANTAYANA

God makes the world all over again
whenever a little child is born.

JEAN PAUL RICHTER

Why Was I Born?

I. The cynic replies: "Forget it! It is a waste of time to try to answer the question. Anyhow, what difference does it make?" It makes no difference? My honest response to this query determines how I live, what I think, where I go, and the place I try to fill in the world. My answer embodies my philosophy of life, and my philosophy of life is just about the most important thing in my world. It makes all the difference between saint and sinner, hero and coward, and moral optimist and cynic, for life is crystallized thought. We live by the deepest and dominant convictions of our minds and hearts.

II. The agnostic replies: "You cannot know. The world is infinite and inscrutable. All reality is hid behind a heavy veil." This is the answer of an increasing number of people who have not the intrepid courage to take the leap to exultant, assuring faith and are too noble to sink in the mud of despair. So they take the middle ground and compromise, saying. "I cannot know." But life does not stand still and wait for us to prove the most significant things, and we cannot remain neutral upon anything in which our lives are involved. Even declining an answer is itself an answer.

III. The sensualist replies: "To enjoy life." Sensualists insist that we came into the world equipped with certain urges, drives, appetites, and possibilities for their complete satisfaction. They wish to avoid pain, to seek pleasure, to dodge responsibility, except where it gives satisfaction, and to bypass work, except to keep happy. They are egocentric and think of others only insofar as they may contribute to their own happiness.

IV. The pessimist replies: "Fool, your question presupposes an error. You talk as though you were here for a purpose. There is no purpose. Life is a dreary, unhappy affair, without meaning or hope." By pessimist I mean the man who has accepted defeatism as his life philosophy and sees no meaning or good in the universe. To the pessimist evils far outweigh the good, sorrows outnumber the joys, and there is no future to work toward and no meaning to find in all the world.

V. Christ replies: "For this I was born, and for this I have come into the world, to bear witness to the truth." (1) In his sermon titled "Every Man's Life a Plan of God," Horace Bushnell said that (a) there is a divine purpose in every life that comes into the world, (b) God has a task for every man and woman to perform, (c) there is a blueprint for every life and it is ours to find the blueprint and follow the specifications.

FRANK B. FAGERBURG[1]

All admit that in a certain sense the several kinds of character are bestowed by nature. Justice, a tendency to Temperance, Courage, and the other types of character are exhibited from the moment of birth.

ARISTOTLE

When God wants an important thing done in this world or a wrong righted, he goes about it in a very singular way. He doesn't release His thunderbolts or stir up His earthquakes. He simply has a tiny baby born, perhaps in a very humble home, perhaps of a very humble mother. And He puts the idea of purpose into the mother's heart. And she puts it in the baby's mind, and then God waits. The great events of this world are not battles and elections and earthquakes and thunderbolts. The great events are babies, for each child comes with the message that God is not yet discouraged with man, but is still expecting goodwill to become incarnate in each human life.

EDWARD MCDONALD

But the angel said to him, "Do not be afraid, Zacharias, for your prayer is heard; and your wife Elizabeth will bear you a son, and you shall call his name John. And you will have joy and gladness, and many will rejoice at his birth.

LUKE 1:13–14

37

And behold, an angel of the Lord stood before them, and the glory of the Lord shone around them, and they were greatly afraid. Then the angel said to them, "Do not be afraid, for behold, I bring you good tidings of great joy which will be to all people. For there is born to you this day in the city of David a Savior, who is Christ the Lord. And this will be the sign to you: You will find a Babe wrapped in swaddling cloths, lying in a manger."

And suddenly there was with the angel a multitude of the heavenly host praising God and saying:

"Glory to God in the highest,
And on earth peace, goodwill toward men!"

So it was, when the angels had gone away from them into heaven, that the shepherds said to one another, "Let us now go to Bethlehem and see this thing that has come to pass, which the Lord has made known to us." And they came with haste and found Mary and Joseph, and the Babe lying in a manger. Now when they had seen Him, they made [f]widely known the saying which was told them concerning this Child. And all those who heard it marveled at those things which were told them by the shepherds. But Mary kept all these things and pondered them in her heart.

LUKE 2:9–19

The biography of anybody ought really to begin with the words, "In the beginning God created heaven and earth."

G. K. CHESTERTON

The Third Birth

Albert E. Day tells us that he was born three times. The first time was on that occasion when his mother looked into his little baby face and said, "My boy." His second birth occurred when God in all His mercy and love opened up His heart and said, "My son." And his third birth was during a night of despair when a friend sat by his side and put an arm around him and said, "My brother."

I. We are all born in human families, and there are no ties quite so strong as the ties that bind father and son and mother and daughter.

II. Jesus insists that a man must have a second birth. This second birth is the emerging from the womb of humanity into a new and wonderful spiritual awareness.

III. The third birth is at the moment of our awareness of the needs of others and of the solidarity of the human family. We must learn to say, "My brother." No pious claiming of the second birth has validity unless the second birth moves on to the third. The identification of ourselves with the problems of others and a Christian concern for the well-being of all of God's children are evidences of the third birth.

LYNN HOUGH CORSON[2]

I thank the goodness and the grace
Which on my birth have smiled.

JANE TAYLOR

Our Birthright

What does the word birthright mean to us? The definition I read is: "Right by birth; a privilege or possession into which one is born."

And what rights do we have at birth?. . . .

The world does not owe every child a living, but it does owe him access to the things by which life can be lived. . . . That is the child's birthright. Some forty years ago Richard Cabot wrote a book in which he listed four things as the factors by which men live.

The first is work. . . . The desire to be of use, to find one's place in the world's economy, is a part of our native endowment; and the person who is denied it is being deprived of part of his birthright.

The second thing by which we live is play. The child who has no place to play is being deprived of his God-given right. . . . The child with no guidance in play will likely fall into habits of willfulness and wastefulness which will handicap his future.

And now along with work and play, there is a third thing men live by. That is love. We are made for love, and without it we are deprived of our birthright. It is hard to imagine a child born into a home which denies it love. Try to imagine a little girl smiling up into her mother's face only to be met with a cold stare. Try to imagine a little fellow reaching out his arms trustingly to a father who turns away and lets him fall. To be loved is part of a child's birthright.

The fourth and last of the things men live by is worship. . . . A child has a right to that larger fellowship with God. A child takes to religion naturally, and to coop him up in a little earthly cage of material things is to clip his wings. . . .

Our social welfare rests on moral and spiritual values. These belong to our children's birthright.

RALPH W. SOCKMAN[3]

Is this a healthy town?" asked a Chicago man of a native of a certain community in the West.

"It sure is," replied the native. "When I came here, I hadn't the strength to utter a word; I had scarcely a hair on my head; I couldn't walk across the room, even with assistance; I had to be lifted in and out of bed."

"That's wonderful!" exclaimed the innocent from Chicago. "How long have you been here?"

"I was born here."

FARM LIFE

Don Pedro: Out of question, you were born in a merry hour.

Beatrice: No, sure, my lord, my mother cried; but then there was a star danced, and under that I was born.

WILLIAM SHAKESPEARE, *MUCH ADO ABOUT NOTHING*

A baby struggling to liberate itself from the womb reaches a crisis where he, not his mother, has to do the breathing. To encourage the lungs to make this radical adjustment the physician gives the baby a sharp slap. The slap is the child's chance to live.

RABBI ALVAN RUBIN

Our birth is but a sleep and a forgetting:
     The Soul that rises with us, our life's Star,
Hath elsewhere its setting,
And cometh from afar;
Not in entire forgetfulness,
And not in utter nakedness,
But trailing clouds of glory do we come
     From God, who is our home:
Heaven lies about us in our infancy!

WILLIAM WORDSWORTH, "ODE ON INTIMATIONS OF IMMORTALITY FROM RECOLLECTIONS OF EARLY CHILDHOOD"

Obviously, being born is just the beginning.

We cannot imagine the event of birth being all there is to life—nor even birth ushering us immediately into adulthood. A child is born, and for many years thereafter is still a child. Why do we expect a different process in the spiritual life?

CHARLES PAUL CONN

Where did you come from, Baby dear?
Out of the everywhere into the here.

Where did you get those eyes so blue?
Out of the sky as I came through.

What makes the light in them sparkle and spin?
Some of the starry spikes left in.

Where did you get that little tear?
I found it waiting when I got here . . .

Where did you get those arms and hands?
Love made itself into hooks and bands.

Feet, whence did you come, you darling things?
From the same box as the cherubs' wings.

How did they all come just to be you?
God thought of me, and so I grew.

But how did you come to us, you dear?
God thought of you, and so I am here.

GEORGE MACDONALD, "BABY"

Chapter 4
DAY

This is the day the LORD has made;
We will rejoice and be glad in it.

PSALM 118:24

One should count each day a separate life.

SENECA

Only that day dawns to which we are awake.

HENRY DAVID THOREAU

Today Is Yours

Every now and then my wife will say at breakfast, "Let's have a good day today," and we proceed to do just that. You must seize today because it is fleeting, only twenty-four hours that are soon gone by. If you live to be eighty years of age, you will have only 29,200 days. Each of them therefore, is a precious fragment of a gift called time, your time. It only makes sense to use every day well. Today is yours. Use it well.

NORMAN VINCENT PEALE

A Day in Your Life

If you are an adult weighing about 175 pounds, in 14 hours:

Your heart beats 103,689 times.
Your blood travels 168,000,000 miles.
You breathe 23,040 times.
You inhale 438 cubic feet of air.
You eat 3 1/4 pounds of food.
You drink 2.9 pounds of liquids.
You lose in weight 7.8 pounds of waste.
You perspire 1.43 pints.
You give off 2.6 degrees Fahrenheit.
You turn in your sleep 25 to 35 times.
You speak 4,800 words.
You move 750 major muscles.
Your nails grow .000046 of an inch.
Your hair grows .017414 of an inch.
You exercise 7,000,000 brain cells.

WEEKLY ROTATOR

*Yesterday is a cancelled check—
tomorrow is a promissory note—
today is cash in hand—SPEND IT!*

JOHN W. NEWBERN

Listen to the Exhortation of the Dawn!
Look to this Day!
For it is Life, the very Life of Life.
In its brief course lie all the
Verities and Realities of your Existence:
The Bliss of Growth,
The Glory of Action,
The Splendor of Beauty,
For Yesterday is but a Dream,
And Tomorrow is only a Vision:
But Today well-lived makes
Every Yesterday a Dream of Happiness,
And every Tomorrow a Vision of Hope.
Look well therefore to this Day!
Such is the Salutation of the Dawn!

BASED ON THE SANSKRIT (C. 1200 BCE)

The clean tongue, the clear head, and the bright eye are birthrights of each day.

WILLIAM OSLER

You don't have to know how to sing. It's feeling as though you want to that makes the day a successful one.

The flowers of all the tomorrows are in the seeds of today.

CHINESE PROVERB

The day began with dismal doubt
    A stubborn thing to put to rout;
But all my worries flew away
    When someone smiled at me today.

AUTHOR UNKNOWN

Each new day is an opportunity to start all over
again . . . to cleanse our minds and hearts anew,
and to clarify our vision. And let us not clutter
up today with the leavings of other days.

OLIVER WENDELL HOLMES

Thank God every morning when you get up that you have
something to do that day which must be done, whether you
like it or not.

CHARLES KINGSLEY

I can never remember a day in my life when
I wasn't glad to see the morning. There have
been days that I knew held difficult times, but
I've never not wanted to face the day.

GLORIA GAITHER

This is the day the LORD has made;
    We will rejoice and be glad in it.

PSALM 118:24

You can take the day off, but you can't put it back.

Consider the wonder of each new day. "The supply of time is a daily miracle. You wake up in the morning, and lo! your purse is magically filled with twenty-four hours of the unmanufactured tissue of the universe of life. It is yours! the most precious of your possessions." (Arnold Bennett.)

I. Each day is a gift of God, exquisitely adapted to our human need. It is a new day, not just yesterday over again. We go to sleep tired, maybe troubled, and during the night the wise God is at work fitting body and mind for the morrow.

II. Each day brings us a chance to do better and to make good. It is as though our slate has had the smudges of yesterday wiped out.

III. Each day comes one at a time. Our heavenly Father sees to it that the demands of time are accommodated to our limited strength.

IV. Each day is a solemn reminder that "we are bringing our years to an end." We, too, need to pray daily the words of the Psalmist found in the text.

L. BEVAN JONES[1]

This is the beginning of a new day. God has given me this day to use as I will. I can waste it or use it for good.

What I do today is important because I'm exchanging a day of my life for it. When tomorrow comes, this day will be gone forever, leaving in its place something that I have traded for it.

I want it to be gain, not loss; good, not evil; success, not failure; in order that I shall not regret the price I paid for it.

AUTHOR UNKNOWN

Just for Today

JUST FOR TODAY I will try to live through this day only, and not tackle all my problems at once. I can do something for twelve hours that would appall me if I felt that I had to keep it up for a lifetime.

JUST FOR TODAY I will be happy. This assumes to be true what Abraham Lincoln said, that "Most folks are as happy as they make up their minds to be."

JUST FOR TODAY I will adjust myself to what is, and not try to adjust everything to my own desires. I will take my "luck" as it comes, and fit myself to it.

JUST FOR TODAY I will try to strengthen my mind. I will study. I will learn something useful. I will not be a mental loafer. I will read something that requires effort, thought and concentration.

JUST FOR TODAY I will exercise my soul in three ways: I will do somebody a good turn, and not get found out; if anybody knows of it, it will not count. I will do at least two things I don't want to do—just for exercise.

JUST FOR TODAY I will be agreeable. I won't find fault with anything, nor try to improve or regulate anybody but myself.

JUST FOR TODAY I will have a quiet half hour all by myself, and relax. During this half hour, sometime, I will try to get a better perspective of my life.

JUST FOR TODAY I will be unafraid. Especially I will not be afraid to enjoy what is beautiful, and to believe that as I give to the world, so the world will give to me.

AUTHOR UNKNOWN

49

The most utterly lost of all days is the one
in which you have not once laughed.

Today

So here hath been dawning
     Another blue day:
Think, wilt thou let it
     Slip useless away?

Out of Eternity
     This new day is born;
Into Eternity,
     At night, will return.

Behold it aforetime
     No eye ever did;
So soon it forever
     From all eyes is hid.

Here hath been dawning
     Another blue day:
Think, wilt thou let it
     Slip useless away?

THOMAS CARLYLE

Throw away all ambition beyond that of doing the day's work well. The travelers on the road to success live in the present, heedless of taking thought for the morrow. Live neither in the past nor in the future, but let each day's work absorb your entire energies, and satisfy your widest ambition.

WILLIAM OSLER

*We look backward too much and we look forward
too much. Thus we miss the passing moment. In
our regrets and apprehensions, we miss the only
eternity of which man can be absolutely sure,
the eternal Present. For it is always NOW.*

WILLIAM LYON PHELPS

"There is nothing new under the sun," some wise Solomon has said, but there is always newness to be found in me, and if I am learning something for the first time, then I am Eve in Eden to my soul. I carry within me the dawn of every truth, and Genesis is not past but present every morn.

GLORIA GAITHER

*Enjoy the blessings of the day . . . and the evils
bear patiently; for this day only is ours: we are
dead to yesterday, and not born to tomorrow.*

JEREMY TAYLOR

*The forty-four-hour week has no charm for
me. I'm looking for a forty-hour day.*

NICHOLAS MURRAY BUTLER

Live your life each day as you would climb a mountain. An occasional glance toward the summit keeps the goal in mind, but many beautiful scenes are to be observed from each new vantage point. Climb slowly, steadily, enjoying each passing moment, and the view from the summit will serve as a fitting climax for the journey.

HAROLD V. MELCHERT

It is one of the illusions, that the present hour is not the critical, decisive hour. Write it on your heart that every day is the best day in the year. No man has earned anything rightly until he knows that every day is doomsday. Today is a king in disguise. Today always looks mean to the thoughtless, in the face of a uniform experience that all good and great and happy actions are made up precisely of these blank todays. Let us not be deceived, let us unmask the king as he passes.

RALPH WALDO EMERSON

The secret for living one day at a time is found in the Lord's Prayer. "Give us this day our daily bread." God grants us our living day by day. Though he has much in store to give to His children and though He intends the best for us, the Father grants our provision daily. We should live in accordance with His plan.

JAMES L. HEFLIN

He who allows his day to pass by without practicing generosity and enjoying life's pleasures is like a blacksmith's bellows—he breathes but does not live.

SANSKRIT PROVERB

No man ever sank under the burden of the day. It is when tomorrow's burden is added to the burden of today that the weight is more than a man can bear. Never load yourself so. If you find yourself so loaded, at least remember this: it is your own doing, not God's. He begs you to leave the future to him, and mind the present.

GEORGE MACDONALD

Happy the man, and happy he alone,
He who can call to-day his own;
He who, secure within, can say,
"To-morrow, do thy worst; for I have lived to-day.
Be fair or foul, or rain or shine,
The joys I have possessed, in spite of fate, are mine.
Not heaven itself upon the past has power,
But what has been, and I have had my hour."

HORACE (TRANSLATED BY JOHN DRYDEN)

Live for today. Multitudes of people have failed to live for today. They have spent their lives reaching for the future. What they have had within their grasp today they have missed entirely, because only the future has intrigued them . . . and the first thing they knew the future became the past. . . . Too late had they come to that realization, and when finally it dawned upon them, they realized that life upon this earth was very fleeting and they realized the truth of the observation that "A thousand years are as but a day."

WILLIAM ALLEN WHITE

Make each day count, but don't count each day.

The deeper men go into life, the deeper is their conviction that this life is not all. It is an "unfinished symphony." A day may round out an insect's life, and a bird or a beast needs no tomorrow. Not so with him who knows that he is related to God and has felt "the power of an endless life."

HENRY WARD BEECHER

What a wonder it is—this miracle that happens every day and every hour! Only, the unusual strikes us more. God is always doing wonders.

GEORGE MACDONALD

The Singing Day

When the sky is gloomy
    And the world is gray,
When the rain is pouring,
    That's my singing day!

Courage is not needed
    To sing when life is gay,
But when troubles gather,
    Be that your singing day!

SHAEMAS O'SHEEL

Each day of your life as soon as you open your eyes in the morning, you can square away for a happy and successful day. It's the mood and the purpose at the inception of each day that are the important facts in charting your course for the day. We can always square away for a fresh start, no matter what the past has been. It's today that is the paramount problem always. Yesterday is but history.

GEORGE MATTHEW ADAMS

The best preparation for the future is the present well seen to, the last duty done.

GEORGE MACDONALD

Count that day lost whose low descending sun;
Views from thy hand no worthy action done.

AUTHOR UNKNOWN

Finish every day and be done with it. You have done what you could. Some blunders and absurdities no doubt crept in; forget them as soon as you can. Tomorrow is a new day; begin it well and serenely and with too high a spirit to be cumbered with your old nonsense. This day is all that is good and fair. It is too dear, with its hopes and invitations, to waste a moment on yesterdays.

RALPH WALDO EMERSON

Human beings cannot blot out their memories any more than they can refrain from fearing the future at times. But we can grab the reins of our minds and say, "Whoa, I have today on my hands now; My present obligation is to live it well." Sir William Osier, the great Christian physician, used to talk about living in "day-tight" compartments. He said that we need to undress our souls at night like we do our bodies. Alcoholics Anonymous members talk about beginning the day by praying to God and saying, "I may drink the rest of my life; I cannot promise; but today, help me to stay completely free of drink this day." Then, at the close of the day, they thank Him for victory.

This is what great Christians have always done. They live in a state of constant responsibility. Others may take time out, declare moral holidays, make exceptions, but we know that to do so is to turn our backs upon God and to regress. God must work through us. But He does so as we acknowledge at any given time that we are "under God" and must depend upon His help.

Just before Jesus went back to the Father, Peter pointed to John and said, "Master, what about this man? What do you want him to do?" Jesus was almost severe when He answered, in effect, "If it is my will that he stay on this earth until I come again, what is that to you? You follow me for yourself!" (John 21:20–23). It is the old story of thinking of finding God's will in a long-range life program. What He says to us is that if we would find His will it must be in the proper management of our lives one day at a time.

L. LOFTON HUDSON

If you sit down at set of sun
And count the acts that you have done,
　　And, counting find
One self-denying deed, one word
That eased the heart of him who heard;
　　One glance most kind,
That fell like sunshine where it went—
Then you may count that day well spent.
But if, through all the livelong day,
You've cheered no heart, by yea or nay—
　　If, through it all
You've nothing done that you can trace
That brought the sunshine to one face—
　　No act most small
That helped some soul and nothing cost
Then count that day as worse than lost.

GEORGE ELIOT, "COUNT THAT DAY LOST"

Sum up at night what thou hast done by day, and in the morning what thou hast to do; dress and undress thy soul; mark the decay or growth of it. If with thy watch, that too be down, then wind up both. Since thou shalt be most surely judged, make thine accounts agree.

GEORGE HERBERT

Nobody but God would dare to make a day, even if he knew how. Think of the stupendous drama represented by a single day's experience—its thunder of laughter and its oceans of tears, its madcap merriment and its heart-breaking miseries, its new exhibition of human goodness and gentleness and chivalry, its sinister revelation of human hatred and bitterness and shame! Then ask yourself: Would I, if I had the power, take the responsibility of drawing the curtains of another dawn, of opening the gates of another day? Would I dare to plunge the world into such a quagmire of terrific possibilities? Unless I felt that I was strong enough to keep a firm controlling and restraining hand on the day that I was making, I should be afraid to create even the sunniest day. I should tremble lest the day that I had made should be a day of uttermost disaster. . . . I should be afraid lest, on the day that I had made, all the song should be hushed into silence and be succeeded by a universal scream.

God dares to manufacture days because He knows that He is mighty enough to control them with a firm unwavering hand. And, that being so, I need never be dismayed. Since He makes the day, the good must immeasurably outweigh the ill, the love must be incalculably greater than the hate, the smiles must be far more numerous than the tears. Even the tears are but part of the intricate process by which He prepares the smiles of a day that is yet in the making. He does not make days that He cannot control. He does not make days that are not worth making. If He fashions one day to be a day of anguish and of travail, it is only that the next may be a day of glorious birth. When He makes His days, He leaves nothing to chance. There is, about each of His new days, the witchery of the unexplored. It inflames my curiosity. It appeals to my sense of the undiscovered. It is a packet of surprises. It comes, grey and unpretentious, but it invariably brings its own thrills and sensations and astonishments. It is a slice of infinity. It tingles with the unexpected. And so it will be to the last.

F. W. BOREHAM[2]

Chapter 5
(TO) YOU!

Who is it that says most? which can say more
Than this rich praise,—that you alone are you?

WILLIAM SHAKESPEARE

The Illinois pastor Harold B. Walker tells the story of a little girl playing in the sand alone.

A neighbor called over the fence, "Where's your mother?"

"She's asleep."

"Where's your little brother?"

"He's asleep, too."

Asked the neighbor, "Aren't you lonesome, playing all by yourself?"

"No," said the little girl, "I like me."

Be thankful not only that you are an individual but also that others are different. The world needs all kinds, but it also needs to respect and use that individuality.

DONALD A. LAIRD

Therefore humble yourselves under the mighty hand of God, that He may exalt you in due time, casting all your care upon Him, for He cares for you.

1 PETER 5:6–7

*Do not wish to be anything but what you
are, and try to be that perfectly.*

SAINT FRANCIS DE SALES

Oft times nothing profits more
Than self-esteem, grounded on just and right.

JOHN MILTON, *PARADISE LOST*

You Tell What You Are

You tell on yourself by the friends you seek,
By the very manner in which you speak;
By the way you employ your leisure time,
By the use you make of dollar and dime.

You tell what you are by the things you wear,
By the spirit in which your burdens you bear;
By the kind of things at which you laugh,
By the records you play on the phonograph.

You tell what you are by the way you walk,
By the things of which you delight to talk;
By the manner in which you bear defeat,
By so simple a thing as how you eat.

By the books you choose from the well-filled
      shelf—
In these ways, and more, you tell on yourself.
So there's really no particle of sense
In an effort to keep up false pretense.

AUTHOR UNKNOWN

A tragedy of life is being possessed by something that isn't worth being possessed by, belonging to something that drags you down rather than lifts you up, that scatters your life instead of gathers it together. What makes your life great is being possessed by something worth being possessed by, something which lifts you up out of your little self and gathers your life together. You should so live for it that when people think of you, they think of it; and when they think of it, they think of you. The question is not whether you belong to something, but what that something will be or is.

JOHN HOMER MILLER

If you learn to minimize your flaws and build on your talents you will gradually find you are coming to respect yourself more and more because you are an individual person, and not because you are as good as someone else or are like someone else. Attaining self-confidence, based upon real self-respect, is a lifetime process.

C. GILBERT WRENN

How to Be Liked

Lord Chesterfield once told his son: "Those whom you can make like themselves better will, I promise you, like you very well." What father ever gave his son a more precious nugget of wisdom! Seize upon this truth as if it were meant for you. Hang this thought high on the most sun-lit wall of your mind. Use it persistently until it becomes a normal part of your personality.

Men and women—all men and women—are starved for encouragement. Under the warm rain of sincere praise they blossom—in ways that astonish even themselves. Give every person you can, whatever self-assurance you can. Don't flatter; recognize. Help others believe in themselves, by believing in them yourself. You will never know, probably, what a spiritual lift you are giving them.

Yes, indeed. If you can make people like themselves better they will like you better.

THE LITTLE GAZETTE

To me, through every season dearest;
   In every scene, by day, by night,
Thou, present to my mind appearest
   A quenchless star, forever bright;
   My solitary sole delight:
Where'er I am, by shore, at sea,
I think of thee.

DAVID MACBETH MOIR

*Laugh at yourself first, before
anybody else can.*

ELSA MAXWELL

Be bold in what you stand for, but careful in what you fall for.

He who knows others is clever, but he who knows himself is enlightened.

FROM SOMEONE WISE

I have two sons—with similar gifts but very different personalities. What a mistake it would be to try to make the younger brother into the older or the other way around (or worse yet, to try to make them both into little clones of us)! And what a unique treasure God has given us in each of them!

This is true of every person we know or see or encounter. Each of us is a one-of-a-kind masterpiece designed by God the Father.

CLAIRE CLONINGER

I believe that if you think about disaster, you will get it. Brood about death and you hasten your demise. Think positively and masterfully, with confidence and faith, and life becomes more secure, more fraught with action, richer in achievement and experience.

EDDIE RICKENBACKER

Understanding

If I knew you and you knew me;
>If both of us could clearly see,
And with an inner sight divine,
>The meaning of your heart and mine.
I'm sure that we should differ less;
>And clasp our hands in friendliness;
Our thoughts would pleasantly agree,
>If I knew you and you knew me.

If I knew you and you knew me,
>As each one knows his own self, we
Could look each other in the face,
>And see therein a truer grace
Life has so many hidden woes,
>So many thorns for every rose,
The "Why" of things our hearts would see
>If I knew you and you knew me.

NIXON WATERMAN

This above all: to thine own self be true
And it must follow, as the night the day,
Thou canst not then be false to any man.

WILLIAM SHAKESPEARE, *HAMLET*

If you believe in God, it is not too difficult to believe that he is concerned about the universe and all the events on this earth. But the really staggering message of the Bible is that this same God cares deeply about you and your identity and the events of your life.

BRUCE LARSON

Give the best you have received from the past to the best that you may come to know in the future.

Accept life daily not as a cup to be drained but as a chalice to be filled with whatsoever things are honest, pure, lovely, and of good report.

Making a living is best undertaken as a part of the more important business of making a life.

Every now and again take a good look at something not made with hands—a mountain, a star, the turn of a stream. There will come to you wisdom and patience and solace and, above all, the assurance that you are not alone in the world.

SIDNEY LOVETT

The most distinctive mark of a cultured mind is the ability to take another's point of view, to put oneself in another's place, and see life and its problems from a point of view different from one's own. To be willing to test a new idea; to be able to live on the edge of difference in all matters intellectually; to examine without heat the burning question of the day; to have imaginative sympathy, openness and flexibility of mind, steadiness and poise of feeling, cool calmness of judgment, is to have culture.

ARTHUR H. R. FAIRCHILD

How Big Is One?

In the face of global problems and titanic questions, how important is one person? . . . The American concept of bigness has affected our private lives and thinking. . . . Mergers, huge corporations, supermarkets and newspaper chains make individual enterprise and individual taste difficult. We enjoy the benefits of mass production but we are uneasy and even rebellious when "consolidations grow to the size of a giant octopus." Huge aggregations of power exert pressures that are difficult to resist. What can one person do to improve conditions? How much can an individual accomplish for honesty and peace, or in feeding the other half of the world's population who go to bed hungry every night?

God declares that one person is more important and more valuable than systems, corporations or cartels, which so frequently ignore, minimize or ruthlessly trample individuals. Christ's action in feeding the hungry thousands is a picture of the divine attitude toward "little people," toward the one among many. He used the small boy's small contribution. In His teaching Jesus always stressed the importance of the individual. No man is an island, and apart from others we cannot realize our utmost. Community is God's will. Private religion is not the religion of the Bible. But one lost sheep, one lost coin or one lost boy justifies any sacrifice necessary to find and restore. "God so loved the world"—a world of persons.

DAVID A. MACLENNAN[1]

Two kinds of people please God—the ones who serve Him with all their hearts because they know Him; the ones who seek Him with all their hearts because they know Him not.

PANIN

Explanation given by a pupil for not joining in discussions: "I think I'll learn more by listening; Anything I would say I already know."

Make the most of yourself, for that is all there is to you.

RALPH WALDO EMERSON

You give but little when you give of your possessions. It is when you give of yourself that you truly give.

KAHLIL GIBRAN[2]

There are three great principles in life which weave its warp and woof, apparently incompatible with each other, yet they harmonize and in their blending create this strange life of ours. The first is, "Our fate is in our own hands, and our blessedness and misery the exact result of our own acts." The second is, "There is a divinity that shapes our ends, rough-hew them how we will." The third is, "The race is not to the swift, nor the battle to the strong; but time and chance happeneth to them all." Accident, human will, the shaping will of Deity,—these things make up life.

FREDERICK W. ROBERTSON

It Isn't the Town—It's You

If you want to live in the kind of town
    That's the kind of town you like,
You needn't slip your clothes in a grip
    And start on a long, long hike.
You'll find elsewhere what you left behind,
    For there's nothing that's really new.
It's a knock at yourself when you knock
    your town.
    It isn't your town—it's you.

Real towns are not made by men afraid
    Lest somebody else gets ahead.
When everybody works and nobody shirks
    You can raise a town from the dead.
And if while you make your stake
    Your neighbor can make one too,
Your town will be what you want to see.
    It isn't your town—it's you.

R. W. GLOVER

69

Accepting Ourselves

When we whine over our own troubles, we only augment our unhappiness and make other people more miserable. To accept ourselves as we are is a primary condition of personal happiness and progress. . . .

No matter how limited is your ability, take what you have and use it. Accept yourself as you are. This is the road to success and happiness, and the way that leads to eternal joy.

There are diversities of gifts and differences in talents. "One star differeth from another star in glory." We are to accept ourselves as we are. We are to reconcile ourselves to our limitations and harmonize ourselves with our circumstances. The faithful spirit is unconquerable, and victory is in our grasp.

> If only we strive to be good and true,
> To each of us, there will come an hour,
> When the tree of life will burst into flower
> And rain at our feet the glorious dower
> Of something better than ever we knew.
>
> WILLIAM PETER KING[3]

My business is not to remake myself, but to make the absolute best of what God made.

ROBERT BROWNING

There Are Loyal Hearts

There are loyal hearts, there are spirits
    brave,
    There are souls that are pure and true;
Then give to the world the best you have,
    And the best shall come back to you.

Give love, and love to your heart will flow,
    A strength in your utmost need;
Have faith, and a score of hearts will show
    Their faith in your word and deed.

For life is the mirror of king and slave,
    'Tis just what you are and do;
Then give to the world the best you have,
    And the best will come back to you.

MADELINE S. BRIDGES

Your heart's desires be with you!

WILLIAM SHAKESPEARE

Your eye is the lamp of your body. When your eyes
are healthy, your whole body also is full of light.
But when they are unhealthy, your body also is full
of darkness. See to it, then, that the light within
you is not darkness.

LUKE 11:34–35 NIV

Who is it that says most? which can say more
Than this rich praise,—that you alone are you?

WILLIAM SHAKESPEARE, SONNET 84

To discover my uniqueness I must give myself away recklessly, lavishly. For you to become the one and only you that God intended you must do the same. The greatest gift you have to give is yourself. The gift of hope comes from being reconciled to your past, fulfilled in your present, and having a sense of destiny about your future.

The Bible says that if you or I would save our life we will lose it. But, if we would give it away with abandon, lavishly, recklessly, we will save our lives. This is how to become the one and only you.

BRUCE LARSON

Rebellion against your handicaps gets you nowhere. Self-pity gets you nowhere. One must have the adventurous daring to accept oneself as a bundle of possibilities and undertake the most interesting game in the world—making the most of one's best.

HARRY EMERSON FOSDICK

But if you have nothing at all to create,
then perhaps you create yourself.

C. G. JUNG

How do you view the gift of God that is yourself? All depends on your response. To accept yourself positively and live creatively on the basis of what God has made you is the way to joy, but to deny and reject God's gift of yourself is the way to ruin. . . .

"Our peace is in our place," and our place is something God gives without our having to strive for it or earn it.

JOHN CLAYPOOL

I wish thee health,
I wish thee wealth,
I wish thee gold in store,
I wish thee Heaven upon earth—
What could I wish thee more?

AUTHOR UNKNOWN

PART 3

From
All of Us!

Chapter 6
FAMILY

The happy family is but
an earlier heaven.

SIR JOHN BOWRING

The family unit imperfect though it may be is, so far, the only instrument society has devised to produce a human man, beset with human frailties, but with his eyes on the stars. A stronger—not a weaker—family has our only hope for the emergence of the man who can reach those stars, not only physically but spiritually.

CAROL H. BEHRMAN

Nothing is more important to human
happiness than to be part of a fractious,
forgiving, warm, tightly knit family.

MARJORIE HOLMES

For the joy of human love,
Brother, sister, parent, child,
Friends on earth, and friends above,
For all gentle thoughts and mild,
Lord of all, to Thee we raise
This our sacrifice of praise.

FOLLIOTT SANDFORD PIERPOINT

Nothing outside of home can take the place of home.
The school is an invaluable adjunct to the home, but it
is a wretched substitute for it. The family relation is the
most fundamental, the most important of all relations.

THEODORE ROOSEVELT

Home is a place where we can learn by
making a mistake and still not be defeated.
It is a place of the second chance.

JAMES RATHBUM

Everyone either belongs to a home or else wants to belong. Everyone either looks back on a happy home which gave security and understanding of life or else sadly, perhaps even resentfully and bitterly, recalls the opposite. As a result the warp and woof of life are woven around the pattern of our home.

How very much then we need Christian homes—homes from which will flow "rivers of living water" in deeply spiritual lives.

H. W. SUTHERLAND[1]

The happy family is but
an earlier heaven.

SIR JOHN BOWRING

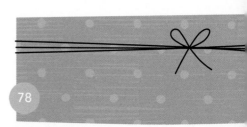

Washington, the brave, the wise, the good . . . valiant without fear, confident without presumption. In disaster, calm; in success, moderate; in all, himself. The hero, the patriot . . . the friend of mankind, who, when he had won all, renounced all, and sought in the bosom of his family and nature, retirement; and in the hope of religion, immortality.

INSCRIPTION AT MOUNT VERNON

Family life is the source of the greatest human happiness. This happiness is the simplest and least costly kind, and it cannot be purchased with money. But it can be increased if we do two things: if we recognize and uphold the essential values of family life and if we get and keep control of the process of social change so as to make it give us what is needed to make family life perform its essential functions.

ROBERT J. HAVIGHURST

Ancestors

Knowing something about his ancestors . . . gives a man a satisfying sense of being part of a continuum, of a process of birth, death and rebirth that started long before he was born, and will continue long after he is dead. And as a man's age increases, this sense of being part of the endless human parade through history is an oddly comforting sense.

STEWART ALSOP

The measure of a man's character is not what he gets from his ancestors, but what he leaves his descendants.

A young man was trying to impress some people he'd just met at a party.

"My family's ancestry is quite old and dates back to the days of King Henry the Eighth of England," he boasted, and turning to an elderly woman seated next to him, asked, "How old is your family, dear?"

"Well," she replied with a reserved smile, "I can't really say because all of our family records were lost in the flood."

The man who has nothing to boast of but his illustrious ancestry is like the potato—the best part underground.

SIR THOMAS OVERBURY

To a man who had proudly said, "My ancestors came over in the Mayflower," Will Rogers retorted, "My ancestors were waiting on the beach."

From our ancestors come our names; but
from our virtues come our honors.

The cheapest way to have your family tree
traced is to run for public office.

GRIT

If a family can meet trouble together and triumph over it, then nothing can overcome that family, and each of its members will be able to cope with his own life a little better than before.

MARJORIE HOLMES

It is always in the home that a youngster develops a respectful attitude toward others. When he respects himself and his parents, it becomes natural for him to show respect to everyone.

WILLA FOGLE

Good family life is never an accident but always an achievement by those who share it.

JAMES H. S. BOSSARD

Let parents bequeath to their children not riches, but the spirit of reverence.

PLATO

Sir Ernest Shackleton, in describing the break for safety which he and his companions made when they were attempting to return from the expedition to the South Pole, tells that he was profoundly impressed with the things his companions considered important, as contrasted with those which they threw away. The money out of their pockets they put to one side. Even food in their knapsacks they threw away. But the things they did not leave were the pictures of loved ones and letters from home. These they carried with them; and in moments when it seemed as though the body needed food, the soul should feed on the intangible inspirations that come from love.

ALBERT W. BEAVER

Life consists of relationships. At first examination these appear to be a million and one in variety. Only a few are basic, possibly five in all: husband and wife, parent and child, master and servant, teacher and pupil, friend and friend. Of these the first two are fundamental and entirely within the family. The others relate the individuals within the family to the rest of society. Yet even these exist in embryo within the home in childhood days. Thus the family is a complete training ground for the roles that an individual may occupy later in society. Indeed, the meaning the child discovers within these roles in the home will be the meaning he brings to them as an adult. Thus the family is the fundamental building block of society.

H. W. SUTHERLAND[2]

A small boy and his sister had quarreled most of the day. Finally the little girl, wishing to stop the squabbling, said: "Now let's act like we are brother and sister."

Happy laughter and family voices in the home will keep more kids off the streets at night than the strictest curfew.

Family life is too intimate to be preserved by the spirit of justice. It can only be sustained by a spirit of love which goes beyond justice. Justice requires that we carefully weigh rights and privileges and assure that each member of a community receives his due share. Love does not weigh rights and privileges too carefully because it prompts each to bear the burden of the other.

REINHOLD NIEBUHR

Family harmony is not something you can achieve just by the asking. Nor is it something that will occur like magic; it is something you must work at. Hold back words that hurt, a temper hurts even more. Treat each other with the same tenderness and kind devotion you did during your courting days. Marriage should be the beginning of a true courtship, not its ending. Renew your marriage vows together now and then. And always remember that the love you invest in each other and in your children is like the rays of the sun hitting a polished mirror—its warmth will be reflected back to you many times.

O. A. BATTISTA

The marriage which seeks to live on only a portion of human experience will find life dull. Those who exploit the social without the spiritual are robbing themselves. Those who seek to enjoy the cultural without the physical or those who seek to make marriage chiefly a physical experience are due to experience boredom or frustration. The marriage which would pamper the flesh without cultivating the spirit will degenerate.

MILO L. ARNOLD

Families that pray together stay together, and families that work together—eat.

We ought to be as courteous to the members of our immediate family as we would be to strangers. Virtually all the harsh, insulting things that are said, are said to loved ones—wives, husbands, children—who will forgive even when treated meanly. Give a smile instead of a snarl, appreciation instead of criticism. Let's treat our loved ones as if they were strangers—better yet, treat them as if they were friends.

SUNSHINE

When a father overheard one of his sons say, "If you do that, father won't love you," he approached his children with these words: "I shall always love you. When you do what is right, I love you with a glad heart, and when you do what is wrong, I still love you, but with a heart full of sorrow."

It is the fatherly feelings in a child and the childlike feelings in a father that reach out to each other eternal hands of love.

GEORGE MACDONALD

Family happiness is not alone in giving and getting but also in forgiving and forgetting . . . there are no hurts unshared, no blessings undivided . . . there come, impulsively and gladly, the little precious gifts; a touch of hands in passing, sweet evidence of trust unquestioned; a bit of praise unasked; a tender kiss at nighttime . . . and where, from hearts by love united, a prayer goes up at twilight: of gratitude for dreams come true, of thanks for one another.

BURTON HILLIS

On Children

Your children are not your children.
They are the sons and daughters of Life's longing
    for itself
They come through you but not from you,
And though they are with you yet they belong
    not to you.
You may give them your love but not your
    thoughts.
For they have their own thoughts.
You may house their bodies but not their souls,
For their souls dwell in the house of tomorrow,
Which you cannot visit, even in your dreams.
You may strive to be like them, but seek not to
    make them like you.
For life goes not backward nor tarries with
    yesterday.

KAHLIL GIBRAN[3]

*In old age the consolation of hope is
reserved for the tenderness of parents, who
commence a new life in their children.*

EDWARD GIBBON

*The test of successful parenthood is the level of
certainty with which children, on becoming adults,
can say: I am a man. I am a woman. I am me!*

WILLIAM HOLMES

Rearing and guiding children can best be represented by the metaphor of raising plants. This should be encouraging, because raising plants is one of mankind's most successful activities. Perhaps the success comes from the fact that the husbandman does not try to thrust impossible patterns on his plants. He respects their peculiarities, tries to provide suitable conditions, protects them from the more serious kinds of injury—but he lets the plants do the growing. He does not poke at the seed in order to make it sprout more quickly, nor does he seize the shoot when it breaks the ground and try to pull open the first leaves by hand. Neither does he trim the leaves of different plants in order to have them all look alike. It is the children who must do the growing, and they can do it only through the push of their own budding interests!

ROBERT W. WHITE

As a parent or teacher we hold a child's assets in trust. If we hold them too long, the result is that the child's growth in responsibility is curtailed and he is immature. If we release them too soon the child is not ready and rebels at responsibility and this also results in immaturity.

ROBERT RHAY

Parents are like editors. The planning for a new child is not unlike planning for a new issue of a magazine. The blue pencil must be used frequently and a rough draft worked on until it becomes presentable copy.

JOHN W. COOK

Certainly we must encourage our son and daughter to do their best, but it must be their best. We have to be careful in helping them set their goals. If too high they are discouraged, if too low they are not challenged. But above all we must help them, the home and church working together, to build a Christian scale of values; so that they will not put first success as measured by possessions, power, position.

W. TALIAFERRO THOMPSON

The parent can train the natures of children to remain fast while their habits change through the years. We must have a citizenry which will by long inner training be able to feel secure in a storm. No parents can raise that kind of child till he is himself that kind of person.

H. CLAY MITCHELL

Older people's participation in our lives gives our children a sense of continuity—a sense of generations, of the flow and ebb of life. This perspective is one that children absorb: A realization that age means experience, that age need not be feared; a dim recognition that parents, too, were once children. Today we have suburban developments where children of young families are growing up without seeing old people as part of their day-to-day living. It seems to me that children need the natural balance of both young and old—and contact with their grandparents helps to provide this.

DONNA LINDSAY

Next to God, thy parents.

PENN

You are free only when you can accept the past for what it is and only when you can accept your parents for who they were. And let it be. Then take up responsibility for your own present.

MARK TROTTER[4]

A parent may be a "daddy" who can fix anything or a "mommy" who can kiss a bruised finger and make it better. A parent may be a father who is big and strong. To hold his hand is to be safe. A parent may be a mother who is soft and warm. She is a place to go to whenever her help and comfort are needed. To a "little one," a "youngster," a "teenager" a parent is a tower of strength, a source of refuge, a ready helper—just about everything a child needs. Everything, that is, except God. Fathers and mothers stand as God's representatives in the everyday bodily needs of their children, but they can't take the place of God. Only a parent can do a good job of bringing God into a child's life. The Sunday school and church can teach a child through educational resources, but the church can't take the place of parents. It can only help parents do their job.

ALL-CHURCH PRESS

Every parent is at some time the father of the unreturned prodigal, with nothing to do but keep his house open to hope.

JOHN CIARDI

Chapter 7
FRIENDS

A friend hath the skill and observation of the best physician; the diligence and vigilance of the best nurse; and the tenderness and patience of the best mother.

EDWARD HYDE, LORD CLARENDON

No friendless man ('twas well said) can be truly himself; What a man looketh for in his friend and findeth, and loving self best, loveth better than himself, is his own better self, his live lovable idea, flowering by expansion in the loves of his life.

ROBERT BRIDGES

He who has a thousand friends
Has not a friend to spare.

ALI BEN ABU TALEB (AD 660), TRANSLATED BY RALPH WALDO EMERSON

Silence makes the real conversations between friends. Not the saying but the never needing to say is what counts.

MARGARET LEE RUNBECK

It is great to have friends when one is young, but indeed it is still more so when you are getting old. When we are young, friends are, like everything else, a matter of course. In the old days we know what it means to have them.

EDVARD GRIEG

Friends are necessary to a happy life. When friendship deserts us we are as lonely and helpless as a ship, left by the tide high upon the shore. When friendship returns to us, it is as though the tide came back, gave us buoyancy and freedom, and opened to us the wide places of the world.

HARRY EMERSON FOSDICK

Go often to the house of thy friend, for weeds choke the unused path.

RALPH WALDO EMERSON

A friend is a person who does his knocking before he enters instead of after he leaves.

IRENE LOENIG KEEPIN

Throughout all eternity—including now—the deep respect and trust of a friend is probably the most satisfying of life's experiences.

WALTER MACPEEK

Friendship, peculiar boon of Heav'n
The noble mind's delight and pride,
To men and angels only giv'n
To all the lower world denied.

SAMUEL JOHNSON, "FRIENDSHIP"

In some respects friends are like surprise packages: you can never be quite sure what's hidden in the outer wrappings. But more than that, there's a challenge implicit in the starting of a friendship that doesn't exist in most other personal relationships. After all, you inherit your family, you're assigned to your classmates, you acquire your neighbors by chance. But a friend you choose to be that: and she chooses in return. The fact is that a friend is often the first person in your life who isn't required to like you.

NORMAN M. LOBSENZ

*Friendship is the only cement
that will hold the world together.*

WOODROW WILSON

To a Friend

I love you not only for what you are, but for what I am when I am with you.

I love you not only for what you have made of yourself, but for what you are making of me.

I love you for the part of me that you bring out.

I love you for putting your hand into my heaped-up heart and passing over all the foolish and frivolous and weak things that you can't help dimly seeing there, and for drawing out into the light all the beautiful radiant belongings that no one else had looked quite far enough to find.

I love you for ignoring the possibilities of the fool and weakling in me, and for laying firm hold on the possibilities of the good in me.

I love you for closing your ears to the discords in me, and for adding to the music in me by worshipful listening.

I love you because you are helping me to make of the timber of my life not a tavern, but a temple, and of the words of my every day not a reproach, but a song.

I love you because you have done more than any creed could have done to make me happy.

You have done it without a touch, without a word, without a sign.

You have done it first by being yourself.

After all, perhaps this is what being a friend means.

AUTHOR UNKNOWN

The first general rule for friendship is to be a friend,
to be open, natural, interested; the second rule is
to take time for friendship. Friendship, after all,
is what life is finally about. Everything material
and professional exists in the end for persons.

NELS F. S. FERRÉ

Don't flatter yourself that friendship authorizes you to say disagreeable things to your intimates. The nearer you come into relation with a person, the more necessary do tact and courtesy become. Except in cases of necessity, which are rare, leave your friend to learn unpleasant things from his enemies; they are ready enough to tell him.

OLIVER WENDELL HOLMES

I didn't find my friends; the good God gave them to me.

RALPH WALDO EMERSON

The happiest miser on earth—the man who
saves up all the friends he makes.

CHEER

We should not visit our friends in order to spill out the sordid, petty problems. Rather, to taste together the pleasures of reminiscence of the past, plans for the future, a shared meal, shared work, shared laughter. Since Biblical days there has been no better therapy than this—for a "faithful friend is the medicine of life."

JANET GRAHAM

Jesus' home was the road along which He walked
with His friends in search of new friends.

GIOVANNI PAPINI

Fellowship kept [Jesus] very near the Father and His pulsating Heart. Fellowship is much more than just talking. Talk is not always a sign of friendship or fellowship. A quiet period is sometimes a good sign that two souls are knit together in love.

GUY EVERTON TREMAINE

If there's a stranger in your neighborhood
today, better check up on him: he may need
a friend. If he's still a stranger tomorrow,
better check up on your neighborhood.

BURTON HILLIS

I Sought My Soul

I sought my soul,
But my soul I could not see.
I sought my God,
But my God eluded me.
I sought my brother,
And I found all three.

AUTHOR UNKNOWN

No life is so strong and complete,
But it yearns for the smile of a friend.

WALLACE BRUCE

The most I can do for my friend is simply to be his friend. I have no wealth to bestow on him. If he knows that I am happy in loving him, he will want no other reward. Is not friendship divine in this?

HENRY DAVID THOREAU

So long as we love, we serve. So long as we are loved by others, I would almost say we are indispensable; and no man is useless while he has a friend.

ROBERT LOUIS STEVENSON

Friends are folks
    without pretensions
Who love us for
    our good intentions.

ARNOLD GLASOW

Make friends and you will make greater progress. Corporations look for executives who are friendly with the public, who have won the public's confidence and goodwill. The way to make a true friend is to be one. The best friendships are born of unselfishness. Friendship implies loyalty, esteem, cordiality, sympathy, affection, readiness to aid, to help, to stick, to fight for, if need be. Friends are essential to success; they are still more essential to happiness. Therefore, to win place and power and honor and happiness, you should begin by assiduously and unselfishly winning friends.

B. C. FORBES

Never cast aside your friends if by any possibility you can retain them. We are the weakest of spendthrifts if we let one friend drop off through inattention, or let one push away another, or if we hold aloof from one for petty jealousy or heedless slight or roughness. Would you throw away a diamond because it pricked you? One good friend is not to be weighed against the jewels of all the earth. If there is coolness or unkindness between us, let us come face to face and have it out. Quick, before the love grows cold. Life is too short to quarrel in, or carry black thoughts of friends. It is easy to lose a friend, but a new one will not come calling, nor make up for the old one when he comes.

AUTHOR UNKNOWN

A friend hath the skill and observation of the best physician; the diligence and vigilance of the best nurse; and the tenderness and patience of the best mother.

EDWARD HYDE, LORD CLARENDON

Thou mayest be sure that he that will in private tell thee of thy faults, is thy friend, for he adventures thy dislike, and doth hazard thy hatred; there are few men that can endure it, every man for the most part delighting in self-praise, which is one of the most universal follies that bewitched mankind.

SIR WALTER RALEIGH

Happy the child that has for friend an old,
sympathetic, encouraging mind, one eager
to develop, slow to rebuke or discourage.

ARTHUR BRISBANE

How many smiles from day to day
I've missed along my narrow way!
How many kindly words I've lost,
What joy has my indifference cost!
This glorious friend that now I know
Would have been friendly years ago.

AUTHOR UNKNOWN

A blessed thing it is for any man or woman to have a friend;
one human soul whom we can trust utterly; who knows the
best and the worst of us, and who loves us in spite of all our
faults; who will speak the honest truth to us, while the world
flatters us to our face, and laughs at us behind our back; who
will give us counsel and reproof in the day of prosperity and
self-conceit; but who, again, will comfort and encourage us
in the day of difficulty and sorrow, when the world leaves us
alone to fight our own battle as we can.

CHARLES KINGSLEY

We do not wish for friends to feed and clothe our
bodies—neighbors are kind enough for that—
but to do the like office for our spirits.

HENRY DAVID THOREAU

Wesley in his Journal tells of a plan which did succeed, although far oftener it might have failed. Two of his lay preachers became close friends, and the one, discovering that the other was careless about money and deep in debt, reminded him that Christians must first of all be just, and added as an obvious plan—"We'll put our pays together and live hard, and what we save will pay the debt."

W. M. MACGREGOR

Friendship

Oh, the comfort—the inexpressible comfort
of feeling safe with a person,
Having neither to weigh thoughts,
Nor measure words—but pouring them
All right out—just as they are—
Chaff and grain together—
Certain that a faithful hand will
Take and sift them—
Keep what is worth keeping—
And with the breath of kindness
Blow the rest away.

DINAH MARIA MULOCK CRAIK

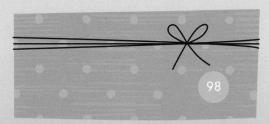

98

For true friendship, it is not enough to have emptied a brotherly glass to each other, to have sat on the same form at school, to have met frequently at the same cafe, to have conversed courteously in the street, to have sung the same songs at the same club, to have worn the same colors as politicians, to have extolled one another in the press. Friendship, indeed, is one of the greatest boons God can bestow on man. It is a union of our finest feelings; a disinterested binding of hearts, and a sympathy between two souls. It is an indefinable trust we repose in one another, a constant communication between two minds, and an unremitting anxiety for each other's souls.

JAMES LANGDON HILL

To the young, friendship comes as the glory of the spring, a very miracle of beauty, a mystery of birth: to the old it has the bloom of autumn, beautiful still.

HUGH BLACK

There is no friend like the old friend
    Who has shared our morning days,
No greeting like his welcome,
    No homage like his praise;
Fame is the scentless sunflower,
    With gaudy crown of gold;
But friendship is the breathing rose,
    With sweets in every fold.

OLIVER WENDELL HOLMES, "NO TIME LIKE THE OLD TIME"

All of us would like to have old friends. But have you ever stopped to think that old friends are not made in a hurry? If you would like to have such friends in the years to come, you had better start making new friends now. Sturdy friends, like sturdy beams, take time to season.

Go at this matter thoughtfully. Select persons you feel pretty sure could be the kind of friends you could prize in later years. Then start the gentle, gradual seasoning process. How? Ralph Waldo Emerson gave us the answer. "The only way to have a friend is to be a friend."

CHEER

Blessed are they who have the gift of making friends,
for it is one of God's best gifts. It involves many things,
but above all, the power of going out of oneself, and
appreciating whatever is noble and loving in another.

THOMAS HUGHES

A true friend is somebody who can
make us do what we can.

RALPH WALDO EMERSON

Nothing in this world appeases loneliness as does a flock of friends! You can select them at random, write to one, dine with one, visit one, or take your problems to one. There is always at least one who will understand, inspire, and give you the lift you may need at the time. Fortify yourself with a flock of friends.

GEORGE MATTHEW ADAMS

Friendship is a fragile something marked "Handle with Care" yet as hard as truth and as firm as faith. Friendship is believing when all others doubt, it's remembering, when all others have forgotten. It's rejoicing in another's good fortune, weeping for another's bad luck . . . It's the man on the road to Jericho who goes where another is—and supplies what is needed, whether it's a word of encouragement or praise, or an invitation to come take a walk on a sunny autumn afternoon.

MYRTIE BARKER

The only way to have a friend
Is to be one yourself;
The only way to keep a friend
Is to give from that wealth.

For friendship must be doublefold,
Each one must give his share
Of feelings true if he would reap
The blessings that are there.

If you would say, "He is my friend,"
Then nothing else will do
But you must say, "I am his friend,"
And prove that fact be true.

AUTHOR UNKNOWN

If a man does not make new acquaintances as he advances through life, he will soon find himself left alone. A man, sir, should keep his friendship in constant repair.

SAMUEL JOHNSON

The best things in life are never rationed.
Friendship, loyalty, love do not require coupons.

GEORGE T. HEWITT

Animals are such agreeable friends; they
ask no questions, pass no criticism.

GEORGE ELIOT

Do not be inaccessible. None is so perfect that he does not need at times the advice of others. He is an incorrigible ass who will never listen to anyone. Even the most surpassing intellect should find a place for friendly counsel. Sovereignty itself must learn to lean. There are some that are incorrigible simply because they are inaccessible: They fall to ruin because none dares to extricate them. The highest should have the door open for friendship; it may prove the gate of help. A friend must be free to advise, and even to upbraid, without feeling embarrassed.

GRACIÁN

When our friends are present we ought to treat them
well; and when they are absent, to speak of them well.

EPICTETUS

Our friends—may they never have to rely on
their patience to remain our friends.

Faithful friends are a sturdy shelter:
    whoever finds one has found a treasure.
Faithful friends are beyond price;
    no amount can balance their worth.
Faithful friends are life-saving medicine;
    and those who fear the Lord will find them.
Those who fear the Lord direct their friendship
    aright,
    for as they are, so are their neighbors also.

SIRACH 6:14–17 NRSVCE

A friend is one who knows all about
you, and likes you anyway.

True friendship is a plant of slow growth and must undergo
and withstand the shocks of adversity before it is entitled to
the appellation of friendship.

GEORGE WASHINGTON

I never considered a difference of opinion
in politics, in religion, in philosophy, as
cause for withdrawing from a friend.

THOMAS JEFFERSON

We take care of our health, we lay up money, we make our roof tight and our clothing sufficient, but who provides wisely that he shall not be wanting in the best property of all—friends?

RALPH WALDO EMERSON

Greater love has no one than this, than to lay down one's life for his friends.

JOHN 15:13

When you're in trouble you know who your friends are and who has been waiting to catch you bent over at the right angle.

I desire to so conduct the affairs of this administration that if, at the end, when I come to lay down the reins of power, I have lost every other friend on earth, I shall at least have one friend left and that friend shall be down inside of me.

ABRAHAM LINCOLN

Oh! Be thou blest with what heaven can send, Long health, long youth, long pleasure—and a Friend!

ALEXANDER POPE

Wear a smile and have friends; wear a scowl and have wrinkles. What do we live for if not to make the world less difficult for each other?

GEORGE ELIOT

One of the great friendships of history is that of Damon and Pythias. Damon had been sentenced to die on a certain day, and sought permission of the emperor to visit his family in the interim. It was granted on condition that he secure a hostage for himself, who would suffer death if Damon did not return at the appointed moment. Pythias heard of it and volunteered to become the hostage. Damon was delayed in his return by natural causes beyond his control and Pythias was on the scaffold, ready and willing to die for his friend, fully confident Damon was providentially hindered. Suddenly Damon dashed into the arena to the genuine regret of Pythias. They embraced and exchanged felicitations to the surprised delight of the king. The king then commuted the sentence of death, saying, as he ascended the scaffold: "Live, live, ye incomparable pair!" If heathenism had such friendships, how much more should friends in Christ be true until death!

AUTHOR UNKNOWN

What was the purpose of Jesus in selecting the Twelve? The evangelist Mark puts his finger on the first reason when he says, "He appointed twelve, that they might be with him." There is something almost pathetic in these words. He wanted friends, he wanted fellowship. He was alone in a world of growing hostility. We see how much he yearned for their sympathy in Gethsemane. "Tarry ye here, and watch with me." This was his first reason in calling the Twelve, that "they might be with him."

W. M. MACKAY

Every man should keep a fair-sized cemetery
in which to bury the faults of his friends.

HENRY WARD BEECHER

What Is a Friend?

An English publication offered a prize for the best definition of a friend. Among the thousands of answers received were the following: "One who multiplies joys, divides grief, and whose honesty is inviolable." "One who understands our silence." "A volume of sympathy bound in cloth." "A watch which beats true for all time and never runs down." The winning definition read: "A friend is the one who comes in when the whole world has gone out."

EDGAR DEWITT JONES

> These are the things I prize
> And hold of deepest worth:
> Light of the sapphire skies
> Peace of the silent hills
> Shelter of the forest
> Comfort of the grass
> Shadows of the clouds that quickly pass,
> And, after showers, the smell of flowers
> And the deep brown earth;
> But best of all, along the way,
> Friendship and mirth.

HENRY VAN DYKE, "GOD OF THE OPEN AIR"

Friendship is one of the sweetest joys of life.
Many might have failed beneath the bitterness
of their trial had they not found a friend.

CHARLES H. SPURGEON

True friendship brings sunshine to the
shade, and shade to the sunshine.

THOMAS BURKE

A friend is a present you give yourself.

ROBERT LOUIS STEVENSON

The Heart of a Friend

Out of the mist comes the fragrance
We breathe in the heart of a rose
Out of the world come the friendships
That brighten the day at its close
Out of the heart comes the kindness
To comfort the hour of tears;
Out of time come gently
Our days, our weeks, our years;
Out of the boundless universe
Comes Divine love without end.
And all of these treasures are blended
In the faithful heart of a friend.

AUTHOR UNKNOWN

Chapter 8
GIFTS

It is possible to give without loving, but
it is impossible to love without giving.

RICHARD BRAUNSTEIN

*To reveal its complacence by gifts is
one of the native dialects of love.*

LYDIA HUNTLEY SIGOURNEY

The best thing to give to your enemy is forgiveness; to your
opponent, tolerance; to a friend, your heart; to your child, a
good example; to your father, deference; to your mother, conduct that will make her proud of you; to yourself, respect; to
all men, charity.

A. J. BALFOUR

*The manner of giving shows
the character of the giver,
more than the gift itself.*

JOHANN KASPAR LAVATER

In 1874, Benjamin Franklin wrote the following letter to Benjamin Webb:

Dear Sir:

Your situation grieves me and I send you herewith a banknote for ten louis d'or. I do not pretend to give such a sum; I only lend it to you. When you shall return to your country, you cannot fail of getting into some business that will in time enable you to pay all your debts. In that case when you meet with another honest man in similar distress, you must pay me by lending the sum to him, enjoining him to discharge the debt by a like operation when he shall be able and shall meet with such another opportunity. I hope it may thus go through many hands before it meets with a knave that will stop its progress. This is a trick of mine for doing a deal of good with a little money. I am not rich enough to afford much in good works, and so am obliged to be cunning and make the most of a little. With best wishes for your future prosperity, I am, dear sir, your most obedient servant.

B. Franklin

Blessed are those who can give without remembering and take without forgetting.

ELIZABETH BIBESCO

Give what you have. To some one, it may be better than you dare think.

HENRY WADSWORTH LONGFELLOW

Thank You

There is a phrase which is not used as often as it ought to be—just two little words, "thank you." We can say it in many different ways, and every language has its own special phrase for "thank you." Do you ever stop to think just how important these words are?

A newspaper published a letter that had been received by an old lady. She lived alone, had few friends, and did not get much mail, but one day to her surprise a letter arrived written in a very neat hand. It was from a boy of sixteen, crippled by infantile paralysis, who lived nearby. This is what he wrote: "Thank you for the beautiful flowers you have had in your garden this summer. The sight of them has cheered me very much."

What a lovely gesture of gratitude! Not only did the boy find pleasure in watching a pretty garden, tended by the old lady, but more important, he remembered to say "thank you" for the blessing he had received. How many of us would do that? . . .

Many people take for granted the joyous benefits which God so graciously provides. What a wonderful difference saying "thank you" makes! The blessings of this world are many and come to us in different ways. Do not accept them as a matter of right. We should glorify God and remember to say "thank you" every day for His love and care, like St. Paul, "Always and for everything giving thanks to God."

STANLEY BARRATT[1]

God's gifts put man's best dreams to shame.

ELIZABETH BARRETT BROWNING

What is the best gift you ever received? Better still, what is the best gift you ever gave? Perhaps you will recall that in each instance, the best gift was one that was tied with the heartstrings of the giver, one that included a part of self.

A little girl who had no money to spend gave her mother several small boxes tied with bright ribbons. Each contained a slip of paper on which was printed a simple message: "Good for two flowerbed weedings." "Good for two floor scrubbings." "Good for two errands." Such gifts are a giving of self, and how much joy they bring to both the giver and the receiver!

WANDA FULTON

Give, if thou canst, an alms; if not, afford,
instead of that, a sweet and gentle word.

ROBERT HERRICK

Gift of Light

Sometime when we are disheartened with ourselves and humanity in general, we should go into God's presence not with a neatly worded prayer, but into a dark room with an unlighted candle, to sit there long enough to feel the darkness, the blackout of hope in a world where no Christ has come, the hopelessness which the ancient world lived with daily, and then to light our candle and thank God for the gift of His light.

ALLAN KNIGHT CHALMERS

The Gift of Time

Time is a gift of God, the Lord of time. Our times are in His hand. The trouble is, we have forgotten how to accept time as a gift. No sooner do we receive a calendar than we make appointments and set deadlines. It is a subtle revelation of our pride that we make more appointments than we can keep, set more deadlines than we can meet. Thus the calendar becomes a source of pressure and anxiety, and time becomes a slavedriver's whip instead of a Father's gift.

ALBERT CURRY WINN

Happiness is not so much in having or sharing. We make a living by what we get, but we make a life by what we give.

NORMAN MACEWAN

A lasting gift to a child is the gift of a parent's listening ear—and heart.

At Christmastime, teacher Elizabeth M. Allen of High Point, North Carolina, asked her class of fifth graders to answer this question: "If you could give any gift you wanted to, what would you give and to whom?" Here are some of the responses her students wrote.

The gift I would most like to give would be love. It lasts forever and never grows dull. It can be given to anyone that you like.—John Brandon

If I could give one gift I would give it to my parents. . . . I
would give anything in this world if they would live together. . . . —Fonda Hunter

I would give a small orphan child friendship, fun and a home
where he would be happy. I would tell him never to be
sad.—Amanda Greene

I would give jobs and good homes to the poor and stop poverty all over the world.—Laurie Kerr

I would like to give happiness to the people that have not
smiled.—Larry Shaw

If I had one gift, I would give it to my mother. I would give her
a washer and dryer. Because I love her, and she works too
hard.—Darlene Byrd

I would give my crippled grandmother the power to walk. She
stays alone down in her home in South Carolina. We left
our dog down there to keep her company. She seems real
happy when we come; but she gets sad when we leave.
She stayed two years in our house, but she wanted to go
back home, because she thinks she is too much trouble;
but she's not.—Sylvia Johnston

THE GUIDEPOSTS CHRISTMAS TREASURY[2]

Get all you can without hurting your soul, your body, or your
neighbor. Save all you can, cutting off every needless expense.
Give all you can. Be glad to give, and ready to distribute; laying up in store for yourselves a good foundation against the
time to come, that you may attain eternal life.

JOHN WESLEY

One must be poor to know the luxury of giving.

GEORGE ELIOT

*They who give have all things; they
who withhold have nothing.*

HINDU PROVERB

We can give only what we have to give. We can write out a check for a good cause only if we have money in the bank to cover the check. And in like fashion we can give understanding only if we have understanding. We can give a contagious sense of the heights and depths of life only if we have earned, and have in our possession, a feeling of those heights and depths.

BONARO W. OVERSTREET

O Lord, who lends me life, lend me a heart
replete with thankfulness.

WILLIAM SHAKESPEARE

*I have somewhere met with the epitaph on a
charitable man which has pleased me very much.
I cannot recollect the words, but here is the sense
of it: "What I spent I lost; what I possessed is left
to others; what I gave away remains with me."*

JOSEPH ADDISON

Gifts Without Season

Lord, I would thank You for these things:
    Not sunlight only, but sullen rain;
Not only laughter with lifted wings,
    But the heavy muted hands of pain.

Lord, I would thank You for so much:
    The toil no less than the well-earned ease;
The glory always beyond our touch
    That bows the head and bends the knees.

Lord, there are gifts of brighter gold
    Than the deepest mine or mint can yield:
Friendship and love and a dream to hold,
    The look that heartened, the word that
    healed.

Lord, I would thank You for eyes to see
    Miracles in our everyday earth:
The colors that crowd monotony,
    The flame of the humblest flower's birth.

Lord, I would thank You for gifts without season:
    The flash of a thought like a banner
    unfurled,
The splendor of faith and the sparkle of reason,
    The tolerant mind in a turbulent world!

JOSEPH AUSLANDER

He gives nothing but worthless gold
    Who gives from a sense of duty;
But he who gives but a slender mite,
    And gives to that which is out of sight,
That thread of the all-sustaining Beauty
    Which runs through all and doth all
    unite.—
The hand cannot grasp the whole of his alms,
    The heart outstretches its eager palms,
For a god goes with it and makes it store
    To the soul that was starving in darkness
    before.

JAMES RUSSELL LOWELL, "THE VISION OF SIR LAUNFAL"

Rich gifts wax poor when givers prove unkind.

WILLIAM SHAKESPEARE

*A gift, its kind, its value, and appearance;
the silence or the pomp that attends it; the
style in which it reaches you, may decide
the dignity or vulgarity of the giver.*

JOHANN KASPAR LAVATER

He was at the fountain-pen counter making a purchase. "You see," he said, "I'm buying this for my wife."

    "A surprise, eh?"

    "I'll say so. You see, she's expecting a car."

Customer: "I want a birthday present for my husband."
Salesperson: "How long have you been married, madam?"
Customer: "Twelve years."
Salesperson: "Bargain basement is on the left."

The best gift for the person who has everything is a burglar alarm.

Her exalted rank did not give Queen Victoria immunity from the trials of a grandmother. One of her grandsons, whose recklessness in spending money provoked her strong disapproval, wrote to the Queen reminding her of his approaching birthday and delicately suggested that money would be the most acceptable gift. In her own hand she answered, sternly reproving the youth for the sin of extravagance and urging upon him the practice of economy. His reply staggered her:

"Dear Grandma," it ran, "thank you for your kind letter of advice. I have sold the same for five pounds."

AUTHOR UNKNOWN

Extending the olive branch of peace—The goddess Minerva was closely connected with the olive tree, having given it to Greece as a gift. She ruled over the arts of peace. An olive-branch gift is a policy of peace.

AUTHOR UNKNOWN

A man's gift makes room for him,
And brings him before great men.

PROVERBS 18:16

Every good gift and every perfect gift is from above, and comes down from the Father of lights, with whom there is no variation or shadow of turning.

JAMES 1:17

When thou makest presents, let them be of such things as will last long; to the end they may be in some sort immortal, and may frequently refresh the memory of the receiver.

THOMAS FULLER

There was a man, though some did count
    him mad,
The more he cast away the more he had.

JOHN BUNYAN

It is the will, and not the gift that makes the giver.

G. E. LESSING

He who loves with purity considers not the gift of the lover, but the love of the giver.

THOMAS Á KEMPIS

The Golden Ladder of Giving

1. To give reluctantly, the gift of the hand, but not of the heart.
2. To give cheerfully, but not in proportion to the need.
3. To give cheerfully, and proportionately, but not until solicited.
4. To give cheerfully, proportionately, and unsolicited, but to put the gift into the poor man's hand, thus creating shame.
5. To give in such a way that the distressed may know their benefactor, without being known to him.
6. To know the objects of our bounty, but remain unknown to them.
7. To give so that the benefactor may not know those whom he has relieved, and they shall not know him.
8. To prevent poverty by teaching a trade, setting a man up in business, or in some other way preventing the need of charity. This is the highest step in charity's Golden Ladder.

MAIMONIDES, TWELFTH-CENTURY SCHOLAR

Giving is a joy if we do it in the right spirit. It all depends on whether we think of it as "What can I spare?" or as "What can I share?"

ESTHER YORK BURKHOLDER

The secret of giving affectionately is great and rare; it requires address to do it well; otherwise we lose instead of deriving benefit from it.

PIERRE CORNEILLE

You give but little when you give of your possessions.

It is when you give of yourself that you truly give.

For what are your possessions but things you keep and guard
  for fear you may need them tomorrow?

And tomorrow, what shall tomorrow bring to the overprudent
  dog burying bones in the trackless sand as he follows
  the pilgrims to the holy city?

And what is fear of need but need itself?

Is not dread of thirst when your well is full, the thirst that is
  unquenchable?

There are those who give little of the much which they
  have—and they give it for recognition and their hidden
  desire makes their gifts unwholesome.

And there are those who have little and give it all. These are
  the believers in life and the bounty of life, and their
  coffer is never empty.

There are those who give with joy, and that joy is their
  reward. And there are those who give with pain, and
  that pain is their baptism.

And there are those who give and know not pain in giving,
  nor do they seek joy, nor give with mindfulness of virtue;

They give as in yonder valley the myrtle breathes its
  fragrance into space.

Through the hands of such as these God speaks,
and from behind their eyes He smiles upon
the earth.

It is well to give when asked, but it is better to
give unasked, through understanding;
And to the open-handed the search for one who
shall receive is joy greater than giving.

KAHLIL GIBRAN[3]

The heart of the giver makes the gift rare and precious.

MARTIN LUTHER

*It is possible to give without loving, but it
is impossible to love without giving.*

RICHARD BRAUNSTEIN

*Every gift, though it be small, is in
reality great if given with affection.*

PINDAR

Man is born to live, not to prepare for
life. Life itself, the phenomenon of life,
the gift of life, is so breathtakingly
serious!

BORIS PASTERNAK

It is no secret that most people do not feel at home in the universe. Made in God's image, with His purpose that we shall be His sons, still we are beset by the incongruities of our situation. Given a faith in the creative God who is never less than His creation, nor lost in it, we may handle the vast expansion of knowledge concerning it and "dream it for a greater God."

. . . To accept God's gift of Himself to us is to come to be at home in God's universe. Acceptance means obedience and to be in stride with His will.

PAUL COVEY JOHNSTON

Jesus Christ is the supreme Example of giving.

GEORGE SWEETING

Beauty is the gift of God.

ARISTOTLE

Giving

God might have used his sunset gold
    So sparingly,
He might have doled his blossoms out
    Quite grudgingly;
He might have put just one wee star
    In all the sky—
But since He gave so lavishly,
    Why should not I?

AUTHOR UNKNOWN

In all ranks of life the human heart yearns for the beautiful; and the beautiful things that God makes are his gift to all alike.

HARRIET BEECHER STOWE

It is easy to want things from the Lord and yet not want the Lord Himself; as though the gift could ever be preferable to the Giver.

SAINT AUGUSTINE

One day, Turgenev, the Russian writer, met a beggar who besought him for alms. "I felt in all my pockets," he says, "but there was nothing there. The beggar waited, and his out-stretched hand twitched and trembled slightly. Embarrassed and confused, I seized his dirty hand and pressed it. 'Do not be angry with me, brother,' I said, 'I have nothing with me.' The beggar raised his bloodshot eyes and smiled. 'You called me brother,' he said, 'that was indeed a gift.'"

ARCHER WALLACE

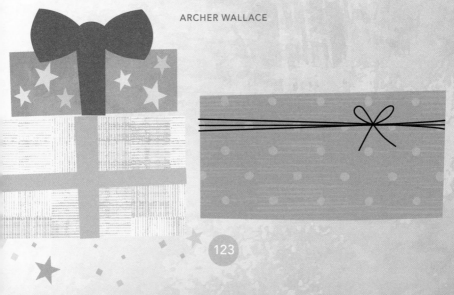

The Precious Gifts

How little it costs if the gift is a thought,
To make happy some heart every day.
Just one kind word or tender smile,
As we go on our way.

Perhaps a glance will suffice to clear
The clouds from a neighbor's face
And the press of a hand in sympathy
A sorrowful tear efface.

It costs so little I wonder why
We give so little thought,
A smile, kind words, a glance, a touch
What magic with these is wrought.

AUTHOR UNKNOWN

*God has given us two hands—one for
receiving and the other for giving.*

BILLY GRAHAM

*The Dead Sea is a dead sea because it
continually receives and never gives.*

AUTHOR UNKNOWN

Of gifts, there seems none more becoming
to offer a friend than a beautiful book.

AMOS BRONSON ALCOTT

Who gives a good book gives more than cloth, paper, and ink; more than leather, parchment, and words. He reveals a fore-word of his thoughts, a dedication of his friendship, a page of his presence, a chapter of himself, and an index of his love.

AUTHOR UNKNOWN

You never realize how fortunate you are
until you enter a gift shop and see how many
things your friends haven't sent you.

Not what we give, but what we share,
For the gift without the giver is bare;
Who gives himself with his alms feeds three,—
Himself, his hungering neighbor, and Me.

JAMES RUSSELL LOWELL

In making our decisions, we must use the
brains that God has given us. But we must also
use our hearts which He also gave us.

FULTON OURSLER

What can I give Him,
Poor as I am?
If I were a shepherd
I would bring Him a lamb
If I were a Wise Man
I would do my part—
Yet what I can, I give Him,
Give my heart.

CHRISTINA ROSSETTI, "IN THE BLEAK MIDWINTER"

To be rich in admiration and free from envy; to rejoice greatly in the good of others; to love with such generosity of heart that your love is still a dear possession in absence or unkindness— these are the gifts of fortune which money cannot buy and without which money can buy nothing. He who has such a treasury of riches, being happy and valiant himself, in his own nature, will enjoy the universe as if it were his own estate; and help the man to whom he lends a hand to enjoy it with him.

ROBERT LOUIS STEVENSON

A small gift will do if your heart is big enough.

Thou that hast given so much to me,
Give one thing more—a grateful heart;
Not thankful when it pleaseth me,
As if Thy Blessings had spare days;
But such a heart, whose pulse may be
Thy praise.

GEORGE HERBERT, "GRATEFULNESS"

Many Happy Returns!

Chapter 9
AGE

We are put here to grow, and we ought to grow, and to use all the means of growth according to the laws of our being. The only real satisfaction there is, is to be growing up inwardly all the time, becoming more just, true, generous, simple, manly, womanly, kind, active. And this can we all do, by doing each day the day's work as well as we can.

JAMES FREEMAN CLARKE

Visitor: "How old are you, sonny?"

Boy: "That's hard to say, sir. According to my latest school tests, I have a psychological age of 11 and a moral age of 10. Anatomically, I'm 7; mentally I'm 9. But I suppose you refer to my chronological age. That's 8—but nobody pays any attention to that nowadays."

Age isn't a category but merely where
you happen to live at the time.

PHILIP WYLIE

The childhood shows the man,
As morning shows the day.

JOHN MILTON

Know you what it is to be a child? It is to be something
very different from the man of to-day. It is . . . to believe in
love, to believe in loveliness, to believe in belief.

FRANCIS THOMPSON

A child deserves the maximum respect.

JUVENAL

Childhood is the kingdom where nobody dies.

EDNA ST. VINCENT MILLAY

Oh, talk not to me of a name great in story;
The days of our youth are the days of our glory;
And the myrtle and ivy of sweet two-and-twenty
Are worth all your laurels, though ever so plenty.

GEORGE GORDON, LORD BYRON, "STANZAS WRITTEN
ON THE ROAD BETWEEN FLORENCE AND PISA"

Almost everything that is great has been done by youth.

BENJAMIN DISRAELI

Youth is the time to go flashing from one end of the world to the other in mind and body; to try the manners of different nations; to hear the chimes at midnight; to see sunrise in town and country; to be converted at a revival; to circumnavigate the metaphysics, write halting verses, run a mile to see a fire, and wait all day long in the theatre to applaud "Hernani."

ROBERT LOUIS STEVENSON

Youth keeps the world alive with its dreams, hopes, and ambitions.

CLARENCE DARROW

In youth we learn; in age we understand.

GRIT

If some way could be found to purge this country of its fixation on chronological age, it would be a great benefit to the way people feel. Animals don't know how old they are. They greet each day as young as they feel. The constant emphasis on our chronological age is a big disservice to all of us. I hate to be a killjoy but we would be better off without emphasizing each birthday with greeting cards. There should be a cutoff point at age 30 after which no celebrating until 80.

HARRY JOHNSON

Never Too Young

Demosthenes was the greatest orator of Greece at twenty-five, and at the same age Cicero was Rome's greatest speaker.

William Gladstone was a member of the British House of Commons at twenty-four. Benjamin Franklin wrote for papers at fourteen.

At eight Beethoven created astonishment by his musical ability; at thirteen Mozart was unequaled.

Pascal discovered geometry for himself at twelve. At sixteen he wrote a treatise on conic sections, and at twenty-five he published a book on atmospheric pressure. . . .

Gibbon, the great English historian, began his studies at seventeen, and at twenty-four was publishing his historical work.

Ruskin was an accomplished art critic, and had written *Modern Painters* at twenty-four.

John Wesley was a polished and forceful writer, and a skilled logician, and at twenty-four he was a professor of Greek.

Moody was preaching at eighteen, and during his twenties became one of our greatest evangelists.

William Cullen Bryant wrote "Thanatopsis" at seventeen. Tennyson's first volumes of poems appeared at twenty. Whittier was editor of *The New England Review* at twenty-three; Poe's first volume was written at twenty; and Byron's appeared at seventeen. Burns was a poetic genius at twelve, and a brilliant and gifted writer at sixteen.

SUNSHINE

We should learn to combine the idealism
of youth with the realism of age, and the
ardor of youth with the wisdom of age.

J. C. MACAULAY

What It Means to Grow Up

Childhood with its carefree attitudes is so attractive
that doubtless we all at times have wished we could
be children again. Certainly we understand the senti-
ment in the familiar line, "Make me a child again, just
for tonight!" One cannot seriously study the problem of
being real persons, however, without encountering the
fact that our neurological and psychiatric institutions,
to say nothing of more familiar places, are filled with
people who have offered that prayer too consistently
and have had it altogether too well answered. They
never have grown up. Their basic emotional reactions
are infantile; they are still in the stage of childhood's
tantrums or adolescent aimlessness; they do not know
what mature personality means. One of the most tragic
failures of personal life is the refusal to grow up.

HARRY EMERSON FOSDICK

A person remains immature, whatever
his age, as long as he thinks of himself
as an exception to the human race.

HARRY A. OVERSTREET

133

The awkward age is when you are too old for the
Peace Corps and too young for Social Security.

The child numbers each day eagerly and can hardly wait to be older. Same with the teenager. But, from thirty-one, one begins to wonder where the years went.

Your perspective on aging shifts. As a child, you thought your lovely grandmother was so very old; but now, in looking back, you realize with a shock that you presently are older than she was then and you are still young, comparatively that is.

If you are "getting along in years" and birthdays jar you, hold your head high, nevertheless, and say to yourself on the day, "I don't care, I am really just one day older than I was yesterday!" And, it's true.

PAUL R. HORTIN

Your age depends on the elasticity
of your spirit and the vigor of your
mind—and on how many birthdays
you're still looking forward to.

EUGENE P. BERLIN

Middle age is the time of life when
work begins to be a lot less fun and
fun begins to be a lot more work.

GRIT

Youth is not a time of life—it is a state of mind. It is not a matter of red cheeks, red lips and supple knees. It is a temper of the will; a quality of the imagination; a vigor of the emotions; it is a freshness of the deep springs of life.

Youth means a temperamental predominance of courage over timidity, of the appetite for adventure over a life of ease. This often exists in a man of fifty, more than in a boy of twenty.

Nobody grows old by merely living a number of years; people grow old by deserting their ideals. Years may wrinkle the skin, but to give up enthusiasm wrinkles the soul. Worry, doubt, self-distrust, fear and despair—these are the long, long years that bow the head and turn the growing spirit back to dust.

Whether seventy or sixteen, there is in every being's heart a love of wonder; the sweet amazement at the stars and star-like things and thoughts; the undaunted challenge of events, the unfailing childlike appetite for what comes next, and the joy in the game of life.

You are as young as your faith, as old as your doubts, as young as your self-confidence, as old as your fear, as young as your hope, as old as your despair.

In the central place of your heart there is a wireless station. So long as it receives messages of beauty, hope, cheer, grandeur, courage and power from the earth, from men and from the Infinities—so long are you young. When the wires are all down and the central places of your heart are covered with the snows of pessimism and the ice of cynicism, then are you grown old indeed!

SAMUEL ULLMAN[1]

Age has nothing to do with a woman's beauty. Perhaps the years can mark you, but this doesn't matter if you are rational in your life. You must change your role. Instead of being a teenager all the time, you become a woman, and then a nice mature woman, and then a nice old lady. Age is not a privilege; it is a condition. You can't do a thing about it except be the age you are.

SOPHIA LOREN

I am—and have long been—convinced that it is when the human being reaches middle age that he really has the experience and ability to savor life, to qualify as and be a connoisseur of the art of living.

J. PAUL GETTY

Tolerance comes with age; I see no fault committed that I myself could not have committed at some time or other.

GOETHE

Forty is the old age of youth; fifty is the youth of old age.

VICTOR HUGO

I'm forty. I don't feel forty. Strange how your body fools people on the outside into thinking you're somehow changing, becoming one of society's stereotypes—an "adolescent," a "single adult," a "college student," a "middle-aged woman," a "senior citizen" or "golden ager"—while all along you stay the same.

I want to shout out from behind the fictitious facade, "Hey! It's me! . . . I haven't changed. I'm still uncertain, nervous, insecure, and hesitant. I'm also confident, independent, adventuresome, and calm in a crisis.

"My body's playing a trick on us both—you out there and me in here. It looks to us both as if I am a mature, middle-aged woman, but I'm a beginner, a dreamer, a hoper, a schemer—a child, a girl, a woman—but I'm alive in here!"

GLORIA GAITHER

I married an archaeologist because the older I grow, the more he appreciates me.

AGATHA CHRISTIE

I like spring, but it is too young. I like summer, but it is too proud. So I like best of all autumn, because its leaves are a little yellow, its tone mellower, its colors richer, and it is tinged a little with sorrow. Its golden richness speaks not of the innocence of spring, nor of the power of summer, but of the mellowness and kindly wisdom of approaching age. It knows the limitations of life and is content.

LIN YUTANG

By all means go ahead and mellow with age. Just be wary of getting rotten.

Age is a quality of mind.
If you have left your dreams behind,
If hope is cold,
If you no longer look ahead,
If your ambitions' fires are dead
Then you are old.

But if from life you take the best,
And if in life you keep the jest,
If love you hold;
No matter how the years go by,
No matter how the birthdays fly—
You are not too old.

EDWARD TUCK[2]

To me, old age is always fifteen years older than I am.

BERNARD BARUCH

If wrinkles must be written upon our brows, let them not be written upon the heart. The spirit must not grow old.

JAMES GARFIELD

Old age is not a thing. It is a process. Or, rather, it is the latter stage of the process of life itself, gradual unfolding of biological events unique to each individual. . . . Being old right now is not at all what the popular stereotypes make it out to be. Most people picture the elderly as poverty-stricken, unproductive, lonely, in poor health, pessimistic, and ignored. Some of these images are true, some partly true, some not known—and many of them utterly false. . . . Actually, the majority of older people are stable, at ease with themselves, less anxious about their health and well-being, and considerably less isolated than people think.

MAE RUDOLPH

If a man doesn't get happier as he gets older, he hasn't learned what he should along the way.

EUGENE P. BERTIN

People could retire nicely in their old age if they could dispose of their experience for what it cost them.

CHEER

Not very far from 70 now, but if I do not in all things, I do in all essential things feel younger than when I was a child. Certainly I am happier and more hopeful, though I think I always had a large gift of hope.

GEORGE MACDONALD, LETTER TO A FRIEND, 1894

How to Live a Hundred Years Happily

1. Do not be on the lookout for ill health.
2. Keep usefully at work.
3. Have a hobby.
4. Learn to be satisfied.
5. Keep on liking people.
6. Meet adversity valiantly.
7. Meet the little problems of life with decision.
8. Above all, maintain a good sense of humor, best done by saying something pleasant every time you get a chance.
9. Live and make the present hour pleasant and cheerful. Keep your mind out of the past, and keep it out of the future.

JOHN A. SCHINDLER

I prefer old age to the alternative.

MAURICE CHEVALIER

I was born in the wrong generation. When I was a young man, no one had any respect for youth. Now I am an old man and no one has any respect for age.

BERTRAND RUSSELL

It's surprising how many people our age are a lot older than we are.

Time Budgeting

As you grow older, more than ever before you need to spend part of each day alone in peace, quiet, and meditation; and in prayer that you may be shown how to continue to live each day with courage, kindness, wisdom, laughter, interest, and understanding. You should take time to absorb and enjoy the lovely world in which you live and come to know its inhabitants with affectionate amusement. You would do well to budget your time as follows: one-half in work, taking care of personal belongings, etc.; one-fourth in social pastimes with others, both young and old; and one-fourth as an interested, pleased observer of life.

WILLIAM B. TERHUNE

Grow old along with me!
The best is yet to be,
The last of life, for which the first was made:
Our times are in His hand
Who saith: "A whole I planned,
Youth shows but half; trust God: see all, nor be afraid!"

ROBERT BROWNING, "RABBI BEN EZRA"

There is a well-known engraving of the sixteenth century which represents an old man sitting in a child's wheelchair, with the inscription over it *Ancora Imparo* (I still learn)— This phrase was constantly on the lips of Michelangelo as in old age he hewed at the marbles and refused to rest.

J. BURNS

As a man grows older he reads more of the Book of Experience and less of the pages of Prophecy.

He thinks more of the real worth of folk, and less of their shortcomings.

He boasts less and boosts more.

He concludes that snobbery is a confession of inferiority, and kindly consideration of others is the hallmark of the only aristocracy worth mentioning.

He hurries less and usually accomplishes more.

He comes to realize that age is but a state of mind and that the greatest reward that one can win is the respect, understanding, and love of his fellow man.

AUTHOR UNKNOWN

To be seventy years young is sometimes far more cheerful and hopeful than to be forty years old.

OLIVER WENDELL HOLMES

A group of venerable citizens at one of those retirement homes was having a high old time discussing their various ills and pains. One had arthritis, another indigestion, a third insomnia, and so on. At length, a spry octogenarian on the fringe of the gathering, cackled, "Think of it this way, folks: it all proves that old age sure ain't for the faint of heart!"

CHEER

The older the fiddle the sweeter the tune.

ENGLISH PROVERB

Never Too Old

Moses was eighty years of age when God called him to the leadership of Israel, and although Moses pleaded for exemption on the basis of his vocal defects, and other deficiencies, he didn't ask it on account of his age. It might interest some to know that octogenarians have made some marvelous contributions to art, science, literature, and religion. Cato, at eighty, began the study of Greek; Tennyson, at eighty, wrote "Crossing the Bar"; George Bernard Shaw has written some of his most famous plays while in his eighties; Scott, the commentator, began the study of Hebrew at eighty-seven; Verdi wrote "Ave Maria" at eighty-five; many judges of the Supreme Court have been nearer eighty than seventy; Goethe wrote Faust when past eighty; Simonides won a prize for poetry when past eighty; Dr. Howard A. Kelly continued to be a world-famous cancer specialist when past eighty. And these are but a few of a mighty host of men and women for whom God found use in their old age.

PAUL E. HOLDCRAFT[3]

Chapter 10
MEMORIES

How precious is memory! What a miracle it is! It can preserve a worthy event, otherwise lost, and then pass it on to the annals of permanence. It can keep unchilled the fine warmth kindled by yesterday's good deeds. Without memory, friendship would not exist. One is educated in proportion to the width and depth of his memory. We solve tomorrow's problems by the aid of yesterday's memory. Great is memory. A psychologist can talk about memory, but he cannot explain it. At the present, at least, it is a miracle.

EDITORIAL, *PEABODY JOURNAL OF EDUCATION*, JULY 1969

Only when one has a sense of the past can one transcend the existential present. Only with a feeling for one's cultural heritage can one face the unpredictable future, the future which is increasingly ours to make.

HAROLD L. BURSTYN

The human memory is a wonderful, baffling thing. The enormous assortment of facts and recollections that even a 20-year-old has had stick in his mind for instant recall would fill many hundreds of volumes if written down.

DAVID GUNSTON

It is through a growing awareness that you stock and enrich your memory. . . . and as a great philosopher has said: "A man thinks with his memory."

WILFRED A. PETERSON

Memory is a capricious and arbitrary creature. You never can tell what pebble she will pick up from the shore of life to keep among her treasures, or what inconspicuous flower of the field she will preserve as the symbol of "thoughts that do often lie too deep for tears." . . . And yet I do not doubt that the most important things are always the best remembered.

HENRY VAN DYKE

We would take from the past its fires and not its ashes.

JEAN JUARÈS

People exist as the sum of their experiences. Memory is to your personality, to your quality as a human being, as your heart is to your body. As the treasury of your past, including all you have read, observed or learned, it provides the color, the shape, sound and quality of your present and future. It is the center, the core of your life. If you cannot remember, you cannot learn.

F. STEPHEN HAMILTON

It is a mark of superior persons that, left to themselves, they are able endlessly to amuse, interest and entertain themselves out their personal stock of meditations, ideas, criticisms, memories, philosophy, humor, and what not.

GEORGE NATHAN

No man has a good enough memory to be a successful liar.

ABRAHAM LINCOLN

According to an ancient Greek legend, a woman came down to the River Styx to be ferried across to the region of departed spirits. Charon, the kindly ferryman, reminded her that it was her privilege to drink of the waters of Lethe, and thus forget the life she was leaving. Eagerly she said, "I will forget how I have suffered." "And," added Charon, "remember too that you will forget how you have rejoiced." The woman said, "I will forget my failures." The old ferryman added, "And also your victories." She continued, "I will forget how I have been hated." "And also how you have been loved," added Charon. Then she paused to consider the whole matter, and the end of the story is that she left the draught of Lethe untasted, preferring to retain the memory even of sorrow and failure rather than to give up the memory of life's loves and joys.

RALPH W. SOCKMAN[1]

Clara Barton, founder of the American Red Cross, was once reminded of an especially cruel thing that had been done to her years before. But Miss Barton seemed not to recall it.

"Don't you remember it?" her friend asked.

"No," came the reply, "I distinctly remember forgetting the incident."

SUNSHINE

When you make a mistake, don't look back at it long. Take the reason of the thing into your mind, and then look forward. Mistakes are lessons of wisdom. The past cannot be changed. The future is yet in your power.

HUGH WHITE

It is only because human beings can remember so much and so well that it has been possible to develop the intricate code of symbols we call speech. The memory capacity of even an ordinary mind is fabulous. Consider how many faces we can recognize, how many names call up some past incident, how many words we can spell and define, and how much minutiae we know we have met with before. Estimates that in a lifetime, a brain can store 1,000,000,000,000 (a million billion) "bits" of information.

ISAAC ASIMOV

A retentive memory may be a good thing, but the ability to forget is the true token of greatness.

ELBERT HUBBARD

A fading movie star, having some publicity stills made, told her photographer that what she wanted was not a photograph that would do her justice but one that would do her mercy!

Each day, in our relationship with those around us, we are making mental pictures that someday will hang on the walls of our memory. It wouldn't do any harm if we tried to do a little "retouching" now and then. Life is likely to be more pleasant for all concerned if we don't allow ourselves to focus too sharply on other people's personality wrinkles, their periods of grumpiness, temper, selfishness, and so on. Why waste film on such details when there undoubtedly are more attractive features if we have the wit to find them?

After they are gone from us, we will envision nicer qualities in our loved ones—overlooked while they were with us—and deeply regret that we were not discerning enough to realize—and appreciate them sooner. The day-by-day pictures you are taking now are the ones that will hang on your walls of memory. Make sure they are the kind you will prize!

THE LITTLE GAZETTE

Think back—often a retrospect delights the mind.

DANTE

A sentence of Paul's might serve as a formula of spiritual progress: "Forgetting those things which are behind" (Philippians 3:13). . . . Paul's sentence reminds us that the "courage to forget" is one of the essential conditions of it. An old proverb agrees: "The way of life is wonderful; it is by abandonment."

First of all, it is necessary to forget our failures. One needs to squeeze out of them all the profit they can yield and then forget them. One may not cease to remember the events, but he can prevent them from becoming barriers to future efforts. . . .

It is sometimes necessary to forget our experiences. We have all known people who so cherish the joy of their personal religious experiences that they never go on in Christian growth. . . . They grow stagnant because of their inability to forget. . . .

It is also necessary to forget our successes. They get in our way at times even worse than our failures. There are people whose horizons are so filled with one great achievement that they never have heart to try something else. Prescott's fascinating story of the conquest of Mexico tells how Cortez was once compelled to evacuate the city of Mexico. Before starting the Conquistador piled the gold they had accumulated in the middle of their quarters and told his followers to take what they would. But he warned them: "He will travel best tonight who travels light." Many of them could not bear to leave the gold behind. But when the portable drawbridge stuck and the men were compelled to swim the next gap in the causeway, many a man found death in the waters because he did not have the courage to abandon the golden fruits of success.

ELBERT RUSSELL[2]

We are to forget the past when, in the words of Dr. Fosdick, it ceases to be a ladder and becomes a leash. Or as Arnold Toynbee phrases it, when it ceases to be a steppingstone and becomes a pedestal. The past is to be used as a key, and not as a lock. It is to be a guidepost, and not a hitching post. Whatever the figure of speech, the idea is that we must not permit the things that have happened in days gone by—whether good or bad—to tie down our affections and attentions, and paralyze our will and strength. The past is something to be looked forward from, and not backward upon.

HUNTER BECKELHYMER

Remember

Remember me when I am gone away,
Gone far away into the silent land;
When you can no more hold me by the hand,
Nor I half turn to go yet turning stay.
Remember me when no more, day by day,
You tell me of our future that you planned:
Only remember me you understand
It will be late counsel then or pray.
Yet if you should forget me for a while
Better by far you should forget and smile
Than that you should remember and be sad.

CHRISTINA ROSSETTI

A great memory does not make a mind, any more than a dictionary is a piece of literature.

JOHN HENRY NEWMAN

Today is not yesterday. We ourselves change. How can our works and thoughts, if they are always to be the fittest, continue always the same? Change, indeed, is painful, yet ever needful; and if memory has its force and worth, so also has hope.

THOMAS CARLYLE

God is a God of memory, giving us another chance because he helps us recall the higher ideals we had in another day and bids us remember the possibilities of our better selves. Memory ought to remind us of what God intended we should be and do, what he still has hopes we will become with his help. And God's help is available. . . .

Our God is a God of mercy. The word "mercy" leaps the barriers of time and tense and is at once past, present, and future. A lady once showed John Ruskin a valuable handkerchief with an ugly blot of marking ink on it. Ruskin asked for it, and after a couple of days he returned it. He had made the blot the foundation for a lovely design. Where there had been a blot there was now beauty, for it had been touched by the hand of a master. Is it expecting too much to believe that God, who "is able to do exceedingly abundantly above all that we ask or think" (Ephesians 3:20), can take our blotted, sin-stained lives and with infinite mercy and skill build those blots into a design of beauty?

J. ARTHUR WEST

*We may trust God with our past as
heartily as with our future.*

GEORGE MACDONALD

*You always remember a kind deed—
particularly if it was yours.*

*Education means developing the
mind, not stuffing the memory.*

Memory Test

What was it you were
worrying about . . .
this time last year?

CHEER

The Grace of Forgetting

Once a boy stood on a bridge watching the water currents go
flowing by. Occasionally a piece of wood or debris would flow
under the bridge and disappear from view. No matter what
appeared on the surface of the water, the water slipped by
as it had been doing for as long as anyone knew. As the boy
contemplated the scene, a thought came into his mind. One
day everything in life would pass under the bridge. The experience of that day was never forgotten. As the boy became a
man, he learned to treat his mistakes and failures as "water
under the bridge."

LARRY KENNEDY

Remembered Thankfulness

Norman Rockwell painted a picture of an elderly woman who had paused to say a prayer of thanks before she began her meager meal in a cafeteria. It portrayed her with head bowed and hands folded, completely oblivious of those around her. Laboring men and businesspeople had paused to watch her, not merely curious but obviously impressed by the act. The picture appeared on the cover of a popular magazine and occasioned widespread comment throughout America. It sounded a note which a materially minded people found strangely appealing. Millions who had been careless in their attitudes toward God were stirred by memories of days gone by when they were thankful for all God's goodness and when they, too, had paused to express their gratitude to the Almighty before they began a meal.

G. ERNEST THOMAS

We live in the present, we dream of the future,
but we learn eternal truths from the past.

SOONG MEI-LING

We cannot speak with any truth or realism about our
faith in the future unless we understand the past.

PETER MARSHALL

You will find, as you look back upon life, that the moments that stand out are the moments when you have done things for others.

HENRY DRUMMOND

"If I had done this instead of that, . . . If I had gone to another school, . . . If I had settled in another location, . . . If I had gotten ten years ago that job I wanted so badly, . . . If I had chosen another vocation, . . . If I had made another investment, . . ." Some even go so far as to say, "If I had married John instead of Henry, or Sara instead of Jane, . . ." Their lives are full of if's and might-have-beens. "If" has no place in our lives. What is past is done, and we cannot change it. Why waste energy bemoaning it, making our lives miserable and bringing pain to others, when it is much better to use that energy meeting the problems of the present and the future? Drop "if" out of your vocabulary once and for all. Instead of thinking in terms of if's—conditional events—or dreaming about might-have-beens, think in terms of actual, new, and concrete experiences. "If" can and will upset your spiritual equilibrium.

WILLIAM PETER KING[3]

The past may explain you, but it doesn't excuse you.

MARK TROTTER

If I Had My Life to Live Over

I'd dare to make more mistakes next time. I'd relax, I would limber up. I would be sillier than I have been this trip. I would take fewer things seriously. I would take more chances. I would climb more mountains and swim more rivers. I would eat more ice cream and less beans. I would perhaps have more actual troubles, but I'd have fewer imaginary ones.

You see, I'm one of those people who live sensibly and

sanely hour after hour, day after day. Oh, I've had my moments, and if I had it to do over again, I'd have more of them. In fact, I'd try to have nothing else. Just moments, one after the other, instead of living so many years ahead of each day. I've been one of those persons who never goes anywhere without a thermometer, a hot water bottle, a raincoat, and a parachute. If I had it to do over again, I would travel lighter than I have.

If I had my life to live over again, I would start barefoot earlier in the spring and stay that way later in the fall, I would go to more dances, I would ride more merry-go-rounds. I would pick more daisies.

NADINE STAIR, EIGHTY-FIVE YEARS OLD

Do not be like the husband and wife who had just had a quarrel. "Come now," he said, "I thought you had agreed to forgive and forget." She replied: "Sure, but I don't want you to forget that I have forgiven and forgotten."

LESLIE R. SMITH

For old time's sake, don't let old enmity live,
For old time's sake, say you'll forget and forgive,
Life's too short to struggle,
Hearts are too precious to break,
Shake hands and let us be friends
For old time's sake.

AUTHOR UNKNOWN

DREAMS

The sunrise never failed us yet.

CELIA BAXTER

*I like the dream of the future better
than the history of the past.*

THOMAS JEFFERSON

There is an old adage: "Keep your fingers on the near things, and your eyes on the far things," It is a poetic way of saying: Give your immediate attention to the tasks for today, but do not overlook the dreams for tomorrow, . . . In every field success demands that you keep your eyes and your mind open to what the future may bring, and that you work hard today with what the present provides. In his instructions to a lifeboat crew, the captain of a doomed ship put it this way: "Don't miss anything new on the horizon, but keep rowing straight to the shore."

CHRISTIAN OBSERVER

*To dream is easy, but to have the dream become reality is
difficult and is achieved only with hard dedicated work.*

ANN POLING

Whatever your past has been, you have a spotless future.

We grow by dreams. All big men are dreamers. They see things in the soft haze of a spring day or in the red fire of a long winter's evening. Some of us let these great dreams die, but others nourish and protect them, nurse them through bad days till they bring them to the sunshine and light which come always to those who sincerely hope that their dreams will come true.

WOODROW WILSON

Some men see things as they are and say, why? I dream of things that never were and say, why not?

GEORGE BERNARD SHAW

To Dream Is to Live

When I have ceased to dream,
God, let me die.
Hope will no longer gleam
When I have ceased to dream.
Dusk and dawn will seem
Fruitless and dry,
When I have ceased to dream,
God, let me die.

AUTHOR UNKNOWN

*The difficult we do immediately;
the impossible takes a little longer.*

AIR FORCE MOTTO

If you're like most Americans, you're too busy to do nothing. And you couldn't if you tried. You'd feel guilty. . . . Great thinkers and great philosophers have always seen the value of doing nothing. There is purpose in purposeful laziness. We need not always be producing tangibles. We can only buy tangibles. We can live intangibles, for they are also known as ideas (thoughts and dreams), all thought or dreamed when someone did nothing but think or dream.

LESLIE G. KENNON

Most of us spend a lot of time dreaming of the future, never realizing that a little of it arrives each day.

When you get into a tight place and everything goes against you until it seems as if you couldn't hold on a minute longer, never give up then, for that is just the place and time that the tide will turn.

HARRIET BEECHER STOWE

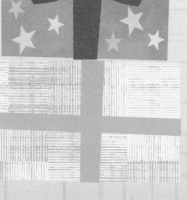

We are the builders who build today;
But someone before us has paved the way.
Someone has dreamed and someone has prayed,
And through their visions, our hearthstones
        are laid.

We also are dreamers today, who dream,
But someone tomorrow must cross the stream,
Someone must fashion from our mind's view
The future building that we would do.
Someone will master because we believe.
Someone will do what we dream to achieve.

CHEER

Some people are so afraid to die that
they never begin to live.

HENRY VAN DYKE

Always dream and shoot higher than you know you can do.
Don't bother just to be better than your contemporaries or
predecessors. Try to be better than yourself.

WILLIAM FAULKNER

How people love an old saying! They are always
quoting "There is nothing new under the sun,"
yet there is something new every day.

E. W. HOWE

*Make preparations in advance. You never
have trouble if you are prepared for it.*

THEODORE ROOSEVELT

Keep Trying

The best verse hasn't been rhymed yet,
    The best house hasn't been planned.
The highest peak hasn't been climbed yet,
    The mightiest rivers aren't spanned.

Don't worry and fret, fainthearted,
    The chances have just begun,
For the best jobs haven't been started,
    And the best work hasn't been done.

AUTHOR UNKNOWN

*To become what we are capable of
becoming is the only end in life.*

ROBERT LOUIS STEVENSON

The people who get on in the world are those
who get up and look for the circumstances they
want, and if they can't find them, make them.

GEORGE BERNARD SHAW

*Success comes more from thoughtful
wishing than from wishful thinking.*

HOUGHTON LINE

160

If one advances confidently in the direction of his dreams, and endeavors to live the life which he has imagined, he will meet with a success unexpected in common hours.

HENRY DAVID THOREAU

Ah, but a man's reach should exceed his grasp,
Or what's a heaven for?

ROBERT BROWNING, "ANDREA DEL SARTO"

The poor man is not he who is without a cent, but he who is without a dream.

HARRY KEMP

If a man constantly aspires, is he not elevated?

HENRY DAVID THOREAU

Be like the bird
That, pausing in her flight
Awhile on boughs too slight,
    Feels them give way
Beneath her and yet sings,
Knowing that she hath wings.

VICTOR HUGO

To fulfill the dreams of one's youth; that is the best that can happen to a man. No worldly success can take the place of that.

WILLA CATHER

There's a divinity that shapes our ends,
Rough hew them how we will.

WILLIAM SHAKESPEARE

If God shuts one door, he opens another.

IRISH PROVERB

*It is well with me only when I
have a chisel in my hand.*

MICHELANGELO

*We should all be concerned about the future because
we will have to spend the rest of our lives there.*

CHARLES F. KETTERING

Hitch your wagon to a star.

RALPH WALDO EMERSON

For man is a dreamer ever,
He glimpses the hills afar,
And plans for the things out yonder
Where all his tomorrows are;
And back of the sound of the hammer,
And back of the hissing steam,
And back of the hand on the throttle
Is ever a daring dream.

AUTHOR UNKNOWN

A wonderful, wonderful mystery are dreams, the life that goes on in the mind, the picture-making power of imagination. . . .

Dreams are the stuff of which life is made. All great things are born there—art, music, books, buildings. "All that we glory in," said Edwin Markham, "was once a dream"—a little picture in the mind. Garibaldi's mother named him, in his cradle, "Italy's Washington"; she whispered it to him in his lullabies; and he came through youth to manhood with that picture in his mind. Beethoven used to wander in the woods to get his music; in the studio of his mind he saw and heard great symphonies of sound dancing, marching up and down on the screen of his imagination. When James Watt's crude steam engine worked for the first time, he shouted excitedly to his friends, "You see it working now with your physical eye, but long ago I saw it working in my mind's eye." That is where all great things begin—in dreams, little pictures in the mind.

Take the dreamers out of history and there is nothing left worth reading about. Columbus dreamed, and a continent came to life. Edison dreamed and night disappeared. "Every great advance in history," said Dr. Whitehead, "has issued from a new audacity in imagination."

J. WALLACE HAMILTON

Life is no brief candle to me. It is a sort of splendid torch which I have got hold of for the moment, and I want to make it burn as brightly as possible before handing it on to future generations.

GEORGE BERNARD SHAW

"They were last seen going strong for the top." This was the last report of the two brave men who lost their lives in the ascent of Mount Everest. No better epitaph for them could be found. It epitomizes the essential gallantry of human striving for the hitherto unachieved.

THE TIMES

Is it yesterday, or tomorrow, which makes today what is? Which has the more power, the push of the past or the pull of the future? Both of these forces are operating steadily, but the future seems to have the upper hand. "Your young men shall see visions and your old men shall dream dreams." They will be pulled along by that which their imaginations picture as possible. They go feeling their way after something, if haply they may find it. They find great sections of it—they catch up with their dreams, and then dream of something yet higher. It is the way of wholesome advance. The future is more powerful than the past, as a source of motive.

CHARLES R. BROWN

Hats off to the past; coats off to the future.

AMERICAN PROVERB

If you can dream—and not make dreams your
      master,
If you can fill the unforgiving minute
      With sixty seconds' worth of distance run,
Yours is the Earth and everything that's in it,
      And—which is more—you'll be a Man,
      my son!

RUDYARD KIPLING

*The most effective way to ensure the value
of the future . . . is to confront the present
courageously and constructively. For the future
is born out of and made by the present.*

ROLLO MAY

*Dreams do come true, if we only wish hard
enough. You can have anything in life if you
will sacrifice everything else for it. "What will
you have?" says God. "Pay for it and take it."*

JAMES BARRIE

Two men look out through the
      selfsame bars;
One sees the mud, and one the stars.

FREDERICK LANGBRIDGE

Everyone lives with unfulfilled aspirations. This gives him trouble with his ego ideal and increases his resentment toward both himself and his organization. Every man, particularly an executive in middle age, needs to take a good look at his yet unfulfilled aspirations. Many times it is possible to do something about them while still remaining in the business. Some start a second business of their own, which also later will serve as a constructive device in retirement. Some take up their favorite charities, some even become part-time ministers, painters, writers and so on. Every man should be working on his dreams if he is to live comfortably with his ego ideal. If he can't admit he has unfulfilled dreams, he's dead on his feet.

HARRY LEVINSON

The sunrise never failed us yet.

CELIA BAXTER

When you have a dream you've got to grab it and never let it go.

CAROL BURNETT

It is never safe to look into the future with eyes of fear.

EDWARD HARRIMAN

Scientific progress is like mounting a ladder; each step upward is followed by a brief pause while the body regains its balance, and we can no more disregard the steps which have gone before than we could cut away the lower part of the ladder.

OLIVER G. SUTTON

The rung of a ladder was never meant to rest upon, but only to hold a man's foot long enough to enable him to put the other somewhat higher.

THOMAS HENRY HUXLEY

Every act of progress the world has ever known began first with a dreamer. After him came the scientist or the statesman, the expert or the technician. But first came the dreamer.

RABBI MAURICE DAVIS

In great straits and when hope is small, the boldest counsels are the safest.

LIVY

It has been well said that our anxiety does not empty tomorrow of its sorrows, but only empties today of its strength.

CHARLES H. SPURGEON

If you have built castles in the air, your work need not be lost; that is where they should be. Now put foundations under them.

HENRY DAVID THOREAU

There is a Hebrew myth which says that when God formed man of the dust and breathed into him the breath of life, He gave man every treasure except one. He withheld from him satisfaction on this earthly stage, condemned him to perpetual restlessness, dissatisfaction and discontent with all things temporal and transient. The writer of Ecclesiastes had a shorter word for it: "God has set eternity in his heart."

I hope the day will never come when the American nation will be the champion of the status quo. Once that happens, we shall have forfeited, and rightly forfeited, the support of the unsatisfied, of those who are the victims of inevitable imperfections, of those who, young in years or spirit, believe that they can make a better world and of those who dream dreams and want to make their dreams come true.

JOHN FOSTER DULLES

Go forward, always go forward. You must not fall. Go until the last shots are fired and the last drop of gasoline is gone. Then go forward on foot.

GENERAL GEORGE S. PATTON

Don't worry about the future—
The present is all thou hast;
The future will soon be present,
And the present will soon be past.

FROM AN OLD SUNDIAL

The vision of things to be done may come a long time before the way of doing them becomes clear, but woe to them who distrust the vision.

JENKIN LLOYD JONES

Every civilization rests on a set of promises. . . . If the promises are broken too often, the civilization dies, no matter how rich it may be, or how mechanically clever. Hope and faith depend on the promises; if hope and faith go, everything goes.

HERBERT AGAR

Hope is a vigorous principle; it is furnished with light and heat to advise and execute; it sets the head and heart to work, and animates a people to do the utmost.

JEREMY COLLIER

Those who have health, have hope; and those who have hope, have everything.

ARABIAN PROVERB

At every moment of time we reach two ways—toward the past and toward the future. Today is always the day toward which we once looked forward, and of which we dreamed. Today is the day toward which we shall one day look back, and about which we shall muse.

HARLEY H. GILL

Not enjoyment, and not sorrow
Is our destined end or way;
But to act, that each tomorrow
Finds us further than today.

HENRY WADSWORTH LONGFELLOW,
"A PSALM OF LIFE"

The way to get ahead is to start now. If you start now, you will know a lot next year that you don't know now and that you would not have known next year if you had waited.

WILLIAM FEATHER

If we are to survive the Atomic Age, we must have something to live by, to live on, and to live for. We must stand aside from the world's conspiracy of fear and hate and grasp once more the great monosyllables of life: faith, hope, and love. We must live by these if we live at all under the crushing weight of history.

OTTO PAUL KRETZMANN

Little progress can be made by merely attempting to repress what is evil; our great hope lies in developing what is good.

CALVIN COOLIDGE

"And what do you want to be when you grow up?" the visitor inquired of the little boy. "I want to be possible," announced the child. "Possible?" asked the visitor, perplexed. "Yes, you see, my mother tells me every day that I'm impossible."

PRESBYTERIAN LIFE

It is not a bad thing to spell out ultimate goals as well as immediate responsibilities. But we must be cognizant of the fact that some people have a habit of fleeing to ultimate ideals as a way of evading immediate responsibilities.

REINHOLD NIEBUHR

Abbie Deal dreams about her new home on the Nebraska prairies. She desires a picket fence around the yard, a nice fence, painted white, with red hollyhocks and blue larkspur alongside it. "You're quite a dreamer, Abbie-girl," says her husband, Will. Abbie does not laugh. She is suddenly sober. "You have to, Will." She says it a little vehemently. "You have to dream things out. It keeps a kind of an ideal before you. You see it first in your mind and then you set about to try to make it like the ideal. If you want a garden—why, I guess you've got to dream a garden."

BESS STREETER ALDRICH, *A LANTERN IN HER HAND*

At the top of one hill the winding road to the top of the next hill looks perpendicular, and you wonder if your car can possibly make it. Yet a few moments later you realize that the car has the required power and the incline is not as steep as it had seemed from afar. Along the road toward tomorrow the way looks forbidding, but the man of faith has at his command such undreamed of reserves that he may move ahead with confident trust.

ROBERT C. NEWELL

We must welcome the future, remembering that soon it will be the past, remembering that once it was all that was humanly possible.

GEORGE SANTAYANA

Don't worry too much about what lies ahead. Go as far as you can see, and when you get there, you can see farther.

Hope

Tis better to hope, though clouds hang low,
And keep the eyes uplifted,
For the sweet blue sky will soon peep through,
When the ominous clouds are lifted.

There was never a night without a day
Or an evening without a morning.
And the darkest hour, as the proverb goes,
Is the hour before the dawning.

AUTHOR UNKNOWN

This wonder we find in hope, that hope is both a flatterer and a true friend. How many would die did not hope sustain them; how many have died by hoping too much!

OWEN FELTHAM

Humanity certainly needs practical men, who get the most out of their work, and, without forgetting the general good, safeguard their own interests. But humanity also needs dreamers, for whom the disinterested development of an enterprise is so captivating that it becomes impossible for them to devote their care to their own material profit.

MARIE CURIE

There is one form of hope which is never unwise, and which certainly does not diminish with the increase of knowledge. In that form it changes its name, and we call it patience.

EDWARD GEORGE BULWER-LYTTON, LORD LYTTON

In the convex driving mirror she could see, dwindling rapidly, the patch of road where they had stood; and she wondered why it had never occurred to her before that you cannot successfully navigate the future unless you keep always framed beside it a small clear image of the past.

JAN STRUTHER, *MRS. MINIVER*

*Excellent advice for those who fear the
future was given by a superintendent of a
telephone company who was instructing
young men in pole climbing. "Do not look
straight up or down," he cautioned, "but
just a little ahead of your highest hand."*

Perhaps the most important lesson the world has learned in the past fifty years is that it is not true that "human nature is unchangeable." Human nature, on the contrary, can be changed with the greatest ease and to the utmost possible extent. If in this lies huge potential danger, it also contains some of the brightest hopes that we have for the future of mankind.

BRUCE BLIVEN

*The search for peace has its high hope
and its deep frustrations. But after the
frustration, there is always renewed hope.*

JOHN FOSTER DULLES

*The natural process of the mind is not from
enjoyment to enjoyment, but from hope to hope.*

SAMUEL JOHNSON

The birthplace of Christianity was the tomb. The birthplace of splendor is desolation. Spring is conceived in the dark womb of winter. And light is inevitably the offspring of darkness. . . . All this heaviness of night is surely but the prelude to a better dawn. The voice of God and the voice of Nature proclaim that the best is yet to be—always, the best is yet to be.

ROBERT CROMIE

Never be afraid to trust an unknown
future to a known God.

It can always be different. That's the meaning of saying the future is a gift from God. It doesn't depend on us. All we have to do is choose it when he offers it to us.

MARK TROTTER

When we build . . . let it not be for present delights nor for present use alone. Let it be such work as our descendants will thank us for, and let us think . . . that a time is to come when these stones will be held sacred because our hands have touched them, and that men and women will say as they look upon the labor, and the wrought substance of them, "See! This our fathers did for us!"

JOHN RUSKIN

Sure! Heart's Desire will come true some day. But you must trust and, trusting, you must wait. You've but to [have] vision to clear the brighter way, and see what isn't written on the slate. You must believe that happier, bigger things are coming toward you through the trying year. Your ears must hear the rustle of the wings of God's glad messengers, so dry your tears! Our trials are tests; our sorrows pave the way for fuller life when we have earned it so. Give rein to faith and hail the brighter day, and you shall come at last real joy to know.

JEROME P. FLEISHMAN

The airs of heaven blow o'er me;
A glory shines before me
Of what mankind shall be,—
Pure, generous, brave, and free. . . .

Ring bells in unreared steeples,
The joy of unborn peoples!
Sound, trumpets far off blown,
Your triumph is my own! . . .

I feel the earth move sunward,
I join the great march onward,
And take, by faith, while living,
My freehold of thanksgiving.

JOHN GREENLEAF WHITTIER, "MY TRIUMPH"

The Lord is my shepherd;
I shall not want.
He makes me to lie down in green pastures;
He leads me beside the still waters.
He restores my soul;
He leads me in the paths of righteousness
For His name's sake.

Yea, though I walk through the valley of the
shadow of death,
I will fear no evil;
For You are with me;
Your rod and Your staff, they comfort me.

You prepare a table before me in the
presence of my enemies;
You anoint my head with oil;
My cup runs over.
Surely goodness and mercy shall follow me
All the days of my life;
And I will dwell in the house of the Lord
Forever.

PSALM 23

NOTES

Chapter 1: Birthdays

1. Reprinted with permission of Charles Scribner's Sons, an imprint of Macmillan Publishing Company, from *John Finley: Poems* by John Finley. Copyright 1941 by Charles Scribner's Sons. Copyright renewed 1969.
2. Selection by F. W. Boreham from *The Blue Flame*, published in 1930 by Abingdon Press.
3. Selections from Mark Trotter from *The Ministers Manual: 1982 Edition*, published by Harper & Row Publishers, Inc.

Chapter 3: Birth

1. Frank Fagerburg, excerpted from *The Ministers Manual: 1971 Edition*, edited by Charles L. Wallis. Copyright 1970 by Charles L. Wallis. Reprinted by permission of Harper & Row Publishers, Inc.
2. Lynn Hough Corson, excerpted from *The Ministers Manual: 1971 Edition*, edited by Charles L. Wallis. Copyright 1970 by Charles L. Wallis. Reprinted by permission of Harper & Row Publishers, Inc.
3. Ralph W. Sockman, excerpted from *A Lift for Living* by Ralph W. Sockman, copyright renewal 1984 by Elizabeth S. Tomkins, used by permission of the publisher, Abingdon Press.

Chapter 4: Day

1. L. Bevan Jones, excerpted from *The Ministers Manual: 1971 Edition*, edited by Charles L. Wallis. Copyright 1970 by Charles L. Wallis. Reprinted by permission of Harper & Row, Publishers, Inc.
2. F. W. Boreham, *Shadows on the Wall* (New York: Abingdon Press, 1922), 73–74.

Chapter 5: (to) You!

1. David A. MacLennan, *Preaching Week by Week* (Ada, MI: Fleming H. Revell Company, 1963). Used by permission.
2. Kahlil Gibran, *The Prophet* (New York: Alfred A. Knopf, 1923, renewed 1951 by Administrators C.T.A. of Kahlil Gibran Estate and Mary G. Gibran), 13. Used by permission
3. William Peter King, *The Search for Happiness*, (New York: Abingdon-Cokesbury, 1946). Used by permission.

Chapter 6: Family

1. H. W. Sutherland. Used by permission of *U* (formerly *HIS Magazine*), 1958.
2. Ibid.
3. Gibran, *The Prophet*, 17. Used by permission.
4. Trotter, *The Ministers Manual: 1982 Edition*. Used by permission.

Chapter 8: Gifts

1. Stanley Barratt, excerpted from *The Ministers Manual: 1973 Edition*, edited by Charles L. Wallis. Copyright 1973

by Charles L. Wallis. Reprinted by permission of Harper & Row, Publishers, Inc.

2. Excerpted from *The Guideposts Christmas Treasury*, (Carmel, NY: Guideposts Associates, 1970). Reprinted with permission from *Guideposts* magazine.

3. Gibran, *The Prophet*, 20. Used by permission

Chapter 9: Age

1. Samuel Ullman in George Humphreys, *Rainbows: The Book of Hope* (Allentown, PA: Coslett Publishing Company, 1946). Used by permission of Brownlow Publishing Company, Ft. Worth, Texas.

2. Edward Tuck in George Humphreys, *Rainbows: The Book of Hope* (Allentown, PA: Coslett Publishing Company, 1946). Used by permission of Brownlow Publishing Company, Ft. Worth, Texas.

3. Paul E. Holdcraft, *Cyclopedia of Bible Illustrations* (New York: Abingdon-Cokesbury, 1947, copyright renewal 1974 by Lola G. Holdcraft). Used by permission.

Chapter 10: Memories

1. Sockman, *A Lift for Living*. Used by permission.

2. Elbert Russell, *A Book of Chapel Talks* (New York: Cokesbury Press, 1935), 139. Used by permission.

3. King, *The Search for Happiness*. Used by permission.

ABOUT THE AUTHORS

Charles L. Allen (1913–2005) was a pastor and newspaper columnist for the *Atlanta Journal, Atlanta Constitution,* and the *Houston Chronicle.* He was the author of more than thirty inspirational books including *God's Psychiatry* and *All Things Are Possible Through Prayer.*

· · · · · · · ·

Mildred F. Parker started working with Dr. Allen in 1968, collaborating in the fields of Christian education and global travel, as well as coauthoring with him the book *How to Increase Your Sunday School Attendance.* She is also a poet—several of her birthday poems appear in this volume. She delights in birthday celebrations for her children, grandchildren, and friends.